Sophie Hannah is a *Sunday Times*, *New York Times*, *USA Today* and Amazon Kindle UK No. 1 bestselling writer of crime fiction and poetry, published in forty-nine languages and fifty-one territories. Her books have sold millions of copies worldwide. Her murder mystery musical, *The Mystery of Mr E*, was released as a feature film in 2023, directed by Martyn Tott. In 2023, Sophie won the Crime Writers Association's Dagger in the Library Award for her body of work, and in 2013 her thriller *The Carrier* won the Crime Thriller of the Year Award at the National Book Awards. Sophie's poetry has been shortlisted for the T.S. Eliot Award. Her poetry is studied at GCSE, A Level and degree level across the UK.

New Poems and Two Plays

Work Experience

Sophie Hannah

CARCANET POETRY

First published in Great Britain in 2026 by
Carcanet
Main Library, The University of Manchester
Oxford Road, Manchester, M13 9PP
www.carcanet.co.uk

A CIP catalogue record for this book is available from the British Library.

ISBN 978 1 80017 555 6

Book design by Andrew Latimer, Carcanet
Typesetting by LiteBook Prepress Services
Printed in Great Britain by SRP Ltd, Exeter, Devon

FSC www.fsc.org MIX Paper | Supporting responsible forestry FSC® C014540

The publisher acknowledges financial assistance from Arts Council England.

Supported using public funding by ARTS COUNCIL ENGLAND

CONTENTS

WORK EXPERIENCE

VILLAIN ELLE

Stories are stories. Real life is real life.
You hint that you might sue for defamation.
It's not illegal to dislike your wife.

Fictional bitch gets stabbed with made-up knife
and you perceive your stab-less situation.
Stories are stories. Real life is real life.

Is 'trouble' just a few lines down from 'strife'?
That's where you're finding risk to reputation?
It's not illegal to dislike your wife.

Traduced ex-friends, from Oswestry to Fife,
privately think she's an abomination.
Stories still stories. Real life still real life.

Discussion of her awfulness is rife
(yet lawful) at Heathrow, at Cambridge station.
It's not illegal to dislike your wife.

I could invent a creature called a Spife
(spindly-wife-esque and prone to pustulation).
Stories remain just stories, life is life.
The law allows me not to like your wife.

FIRST AND TWICE

The last time I was happy, I was watching Francis Hunt
(from the website Market Sniper). He was saying 'Get in front
of the coming wealth-destroying crash.' In words both clear and blunt,
he said, 'Stash some bars of gold beneath your bed.'

Why? Well, interest rates, stagflation and the link between the two,
and the price of debt, the NASDAQ, what a bull is going to do
if some bears jump out of windows, and a Bitcoin surge that grew
then contracted. Then my son walked in and said

that he'd cheated on his girlfriend (on a beach in Magaluf)
though she'd cheated on him first, and twice, but then she'd told the truf,
whereas he'd just cheated once, but hadn't told her, and their youf
and the ever-present drunkness of them both,

and their lay-waste teenage hormones and their strong belief in shoulds
led to swift devaluation of all assets and all goods
and a ruthless razing to the ground of loves and livelihoods.
(Since I couldn't work, I saw no fiscal growth.)

Anyway, the point – apart from: new Black Friday – is that now
I want happiness again, and, what's more, know exactly how
to achieve it: by pretending that the tragic cheating row
never happened. Take me back, please, Francis Hunt.

Tell me more about how hoodwinked libertarians secured
too much tolerance for crypto, which in turn then brought on board
all the risk-shy Stockholm Syndrome types, and everyone ignored
that the booms were just a mirage and a stunt,

and that every fiat system – sooner, later – falls apart
like my son's trust in his girlfriend, hers for him, each mind, each heart,
and I'll tell you, Francis Hunt, how much I wish that we could start
pricing in that human beings are always flawed,

and we do not have to shun them if they slip up now and then.
When we do, we hit rock bottom like, apparently, the yen.
So forgive your loved ones' ill-judged drunken trespasses. Amen.
(And then stay at home and do not go abroad.)

ALEX AND THE SUN

'I just don't want Alex to think the sun isn't out' – Phoebe

When clouds crowd overhead,
look at the turquoise pool
on which a wooden bed
rests like a dream capsule.

The sun plans to appear
at ten, or three, or four,
and it is not last year
We all trust this year more

so each iced coffee glass,
each round we play of *Spy*;
the softness of the grass;
the blue of hoped-for sky

is perfect, and we love.
Nor is there room for doubt.
All sorted up above.
Alex, the sun is out.

SPRUCE IN USE

At Stansted airport, there's a corridor lined with meeting rooms. Each of these is named after a tree or plant. One is called 'Spruce'.

When my exhaustion is profuse,
and all I want is to break loose –
then I recall a room called Spruce
at Stansted Airport. It's 'In Use'

whenever I walk past its door.
That's true in 2024
as it was true in '21.
It makes me wonder: what gets done

inside the well-built walls of Spruce?
What's in there? Praying monks? A moose?
A drunk, cantankerous recluse?
'Don't be absurd, you silly goose,'

my children say. (Well, no, not quite.
They say, in fact, 'Stop talking shite.')
Most who walk past don't ask or care
what Spruce is for, or what's in there.

Tell me the truth. Make no excuse.
Just what the blazes, what the deuce
is inside Spruce? A hangman's noose?
A dead Scots king: Robert the Bruce?

You say a boring meeting room.
That's just a guess, though. Why assume
it's something dull and everyday
and not a Russian émigrée

who briefly dated Dr Seuss,
a bathtub full of orange juice,
a grievance hoarder, too obtuse
to compromise or seek a truce?

I passed that door again today.
Whatever's always underway
in Spruce was underway, all right.
'Hi, Spruce,' I said
then went to board my flight.

RECRUITING MONTAGUES

Imagine Romeo and Juliet
fall helplessly in love, like in the play.
Imagine every single Capulet
then gets in line to shake their hands and say

how thrilled they are, and wish them every joy
as good, sane people do. Who would refuse
to cheer on this besotted girl and boy?
One man and his cowed wife. Both Montagues.

Imagine that the Capulets are cool.
They never once call Romeo a swine,
a cheating weasel or a faithless fool
for how he wooed then ditched poor Rosaline.

They understand: he was much younger then.
He's since matured – and, yep, the crucial part:
he is their daughter's pick, of all the men,
the one who has, and may well keep, her heart.

Dad doesn't say, 'You can't come round for tea,
or breakfast, or a glass of fizzy water
until you've first apologised to *me*
for all that priest and poison stuff our daughter,

our quite-as-flawed-as-you-are ditzy Jules
got thoroughly embroiled in, just as you did.
Nevertheless, we follow despot's rules
and punish you alone. We're that deluded.'

Despot: six years from now, a baby lands.
You never meet her. *Tragic. Blaming. Moping.*
Grandfather clocks – their staggering, ancient hands –
are all you might have left to hold. Here's hoping.

The moral gist is not (as in the play)
that bitter feuds yield only loss and sadness
nor that true love must always have its way;
nor are all fathers steeped in fiendish madness.

Whether you have, whether you haven't yet
found love, as soon as there's a chance to choose,
be, in all ways that count, a Capulet –
ideally, one recruiting Montagues.

THERE'S A POEM I LOVE...

There's a poem I love that cannot be found by Googling.
I've tried with the author's name, some key words, the title,
and there's nothing. This makes it feel absolutely vital
that I carry on looking. There must be someone who(gling)
at some point, on Wordpress, posted a verse or two(gling)
or a photographed page from a long-lost poetry recital.

There's a poem I love that cannot be found by Googling.
I remember the first two verses but not the last.
I've searched right back to my memory's distant past
in the hope of retrieving it all, but only a few(gling)
stanzas emerged. What on earth did we used to do(gling)
before we assumed we would find things super-fast?

There's a poem I love that cannot be found by Googling.
Wherever it lives these days, it is not online.
Should I put down my phone and go to the...? Nah, it's fine.
I'll write this new poem instead. There's too much to do(gling)
as it is – and there's Rightmove and Etsy, Deliveroo(gling),
TikTok, and (retro, I know) Super Mario Sunshine.

There's a poem I love that cannot be found by Googling.
I could ask folks on Slack. But, no, that won't flesh out the bones,
and they'll all be too busy doing more fun stuff on their phones.
They would only say 'Never heard of it. Is it new(gling)?'
If I said it was written around 1952(gling)
they would send the emoji that signifies heartfelt groans,

but it's such a great poem. The bit that my brain's recovered
is ace and the part I've forgotten was top-notch too.
Are you wondering how I know? All I know is: I do.
There were rosaries in the first verse, the word 'solar', and lovers,
And something about words repeated over and over.
(Let me know if this rings any bells. My DMs are open. Thank you.)

AFTER EDNA ST VINCENT MILLAY

My candle burns at both ends -
means I can't put it down.
I'm asking for my money back
next time I go to town.

WILFRED OWEN REWRITES *DULCE ET DECORUM EST*

From The Guardian, 23 June 2022: 'Secretary of State for Education Nadhim Zahawi denounced a decision by the OCR examination board to replace two works by Philip Larkin and Wilfred Owen from next year with a more diverse range of authors, to be studied as part of its GCSE English literature course.'

Rejected, shunned, like beggars in damp sacks
(stinking, with smokers' coughs), we cursed those fools
who run exam boards, who have turned their backs
not just on us war poets, but on all schools
and every pupil who will now not learn
that war is shit (News flash: it still totes is).
Some pipsqueak said 'It's someone else's turn'.
All blame for the ensuing hell is his.

Wait, what? Hey, boys. Hey Larkin – have they told you?
You might not care, but me? I'm glad I'm dead.
Young people: watch out for the lie they've sold you.
The powerful, then and now, they take your head
and stuff it full of falsehoods. Soon you're drowning
in fashionable contrivances, not free

to save yourself. Like Stevie said: that's drowning.
Take heed, Ted Hughes, Lord Byron, Robert Browning –

you will be next. If you could read the minds
of those rank vandals who would dignify,
with the word 'progress', drawing down the blinds
on cultural riches, stamping syllabi
into the dirt; dead poets, if you knew
who they were lining up as substitutes
for (soz to boast) the greats like me and you,
then – as I do – you'd crave a gun that shoots

dead even ghosts. Don't dare say something vague
About letting each new age tell its story.
Have you seen this one? It's all Molly-Mae Hague
And Tommy Fury.

PHILIP LARKIN, AFTER HEARING FROM WILFRED OWEN IN THE PREVIOUS POEM, REWRITES *MR BLEANEY*

'This was Mr Larkin's page. He stayed
high on the list of English Lit set texts
for many years.' A limp-spined book, dismayed
by years of pawing by dirty fingers, next

is handed to you: an anthology
of the crushed hopes and quiet resignation
of English poets: all veiled apology
for wanting anything at all. Our nation,

its oh-so-humble people, are not great
at bigging ourselves up, taking up space.
'They won't print more of those. At any rate,
not with those Larkin poems, though they were ace.

Well, people thought they were, but only those
who stayed up half the night brooding on death.'
'I'll read him,' you blurt out, half-comatose
with misplaced guilt and boredom. Soon your breath

is held while, on the same old shabby bed
in which you write the poems you pray have worth,
you read old shabby words. People have said
Larkin was sexist. Lay him, then, in earth.

Forget him. Whether he anticipated
this slight, who knows? He foresaw most sad things –
maybe not this one, though. It might have skated
well past his range of grim imaginings,

and whether one day a young poet, like you
this morning, will be told that you were dumped
by an exam board thinking it could do
better without you – though your sore heart thumped

with a fierce truth, though your best lines could touch
huge yearnings in small lives – we cannot say,
and shouldn't really bother all that much,
let's face it, since we'll all be dead one day.

MY TWELVE DRAFTS OF CHRISTMAS

Written in 2021, after the government decided to try and cancel Christmas because of COVID.

In my first draft of Christmas, the plan was going to be
a big bash with family.

In my second draft of Christmas, the plan was going to be
two lateral flow tests
and a big bash with family.

In my third draft of Christmas, the plan was going to be
three *Should-we-risk-its,*
two lateral flow tests,
a reduced bash with family.

In my fourth draft of Christmas, the plan was going to be
four *Let's-postpone-its,*
three *Should-we-risk-its,*
two lateral flow tests,
just immediate family.

In my fifth draft of Christmas, the plan was going to be
five star hotel rooms,
four *Let's-postpone-its*
three *Should-we-risk-its,*
two lateral flow tests
and a fun trip with family.

In my sixth draft of Christmas, the plan was going to be:
six *Can-we-swim-thoughs,*
five star hotel rooms,
four *Let's-postpone-its,*

three *Should-we-risk-its,*
two lateral flows tests,
disapproval from family.

In my seventh draft of Christmas, the plan was going to be:
seven Whitty warnings,
six *Can-we-swim-thoughs*,
five star hotel rooms,
four *Let's-postpone-its,*
three *Should-we-risk-its,*
two lateral flow tests,
and a stay at the Iver Langley.

In my eighth draft of Christmas, the plan was going to be:
eight doom-filled lectures,
seven Whitty warnings,
six *Can-we-swim-thoughs*,
five star hotel rooms,
four *Let's-postpone-its,*
three *Should-we-risk-its,*
two lateral flow tests
and a *Get lost, everybody.*

In my ninth draft of Christmas, the plan was going to be:
nine rule infringments,
eight doom-filled lectures,
seven Whitty warnings,
six *Can-we-swim-thoughs*,
five star hotel rooms,
four *Let's-postpone-its,*
three *Should-we-risk-its,*
two lateral flow tests,
and concern for our liberty.

In my tenth draft of Christmas, the plan was going to be:
ten PCR tests,
nine rule infringements,
eight doom-filled lectures,
seven Whitty warnings,
six *Can-we-swim-thoughs*,
five star hotel rooms,
four *Let's-postpone-its,*
three *Should-we-risk-its,*
two lateral flow tests
and a 'No comment' on where I'll be.

In my eleventh draft of Christmas, the plan was going to be:
eleven vaccine squabbles,
ten PCR tests,
nine rule infringements,
eight doom-filled lectures,
seven Whitty warnings,
six *Can-we-swim-thoughs*,
five star hotel rooms,
four *Let's-postpone-its,*
three *Should-we-risk-its,*
two lateral flow tests
and a huge, wild, secret party.

In my twelfth draft of Christmas, the plan was going to be:
twelve *Let's-just-do-its*,
eleven vaccine squabbles,
ten PCR tests,
nine rule infringements,
eight doom-filled lectures,
seven Whitty warnings,

six *Can-we-swim-thoughs*,
five star hotel rooms,
four *Let's-postpone-its*,
three *Should-we-risk-its*,
two lateral flow tests
and a big bash with family.

THOSE PEOPLE

I'm guessing that their table tops are glossy,
their crockery's intact, not smashed to shards,
their garden walls are pristine, never mossy –
though some of them might have white marbled yards
protected by two smiling, suntanned guards –
those people who still send real Christmas cards.

Of course, they'd say, 'What, cards? There's nothing to it!'
They look like us, but they're a different breed.
They'd have us all believe we too could do it
easily – 'Why, you've all the time you need!' –
and if we disagreed, they'd call us silly,
and laugh at us each time we told them, shrilly,
that scoring goals as great as Frank Lampard's
feels easier than sending Christmas cards.

Oh, how they'd laugh. Then, patiently, we'd show 'em
that, though a search for stationery and stamps
would ruin us, we'd gladly write a poem
that's suitable for workmates, best mates, Gramps
and Grandma, all the cousins – just the ticket,
doomed by no postal strike; you just press 'Send',
no need to find an envelope or lick it…
Have a great Christmas! Love from your burned-out friend.

AMNESIA PLEASE-IA

Please forget we have a Zoom;
Please don't join me in my 'room'.
If the gift is in your power,
give me back this crucial hour.

Please assume I'm still in bed,
that my 'yes' meant shake-of-head.
Please work out that I was so
fast asleep not long ago.

Please forget I sent the link.
I have still not had a drink,
hot or cold, since I awoke.
Please decide it was a joke

when I said, 'Let's Zoom at nine.'
Lateness also suits me fine –
not five minutes, though, or ten;
fifteen minutes late is when

everybody would agree
it's fine to say, 'Since it's just me,
I'm off.' Please don't apologise
for failing to appear. Surmise

instead that you have made my week.
I have no time to meet or speak,
which really must (but will not) change,
so please don't call to rearrange.

HOSTILE TAKEOVER

For Harriet Sturdy and Russell Lord

Author's note: in the original version of this poem, the word 'prats' was a different word that rhymed with 'prats'.

If you want to stay at home today, that's quite all right with me.
There's no uniform requirement. Every period is free,
and forget about your homework and your sports kit and your SATS.
Kids, your school's been taken over by a bunch of evil prats.

Throw your Latin book away. The Latin teacher fell apart.
They-a culpa; not his fault. The vicious bastards broke his heart.
Those promoted seem quite perky (ship has sunk, yet still: huge rats).
Parents: school's been taken over by a bunch of evil prats –

that's the most important lesson that you're going to need to learn.
How to deal with evil prats? Do not appease. Do not return
to the lies (yes, lies; yes, even though the prat in question smiled.)
Do not trust them with a sandwich, let alone your precious child.

Don't return with pots of strychnine, hand grenades or baseball bats.
Don't return with hopeful hearts, for platitudes and cosy chats.
There's a truth they'll never tell us (all together now!) and that's
that the school's been taken over by a bunch of evil prats.

CHANCE MEETING

Sometimes I'm still as angry. Sometimes, more.
Do I regret the rift? No, not one bit.
At the same time, my hunch is, if I saw
you on the street, I might snap out of it

without deliberately deciding to –
if I were rushing, say, and you appeared.
The heartening and instinctive thing to do
would be to smile and say 'Hello! It's weird,

isn't it, being face to face like this,
given that…? Well, you know.' What would come next?
Would we both laugh at all the wild boo-hiss
we crammed into our heated, righteous texts,

our resolutions never to forgive?
What kind of fool drops tightly clutched beliefs
for a chance meeting? That's no way to live.
Unplanned collisions rarely trump our griefs

even when we crash into what's as true
as doubts we spend our words insisting on.
What if I dared myself to smile at you
and it's still there, somehow, and it's all gone?

THE MEANS

Lie down. Do not be counted.
Relax. You still exist.
When the attack is mounted
you won't be on the list.

They'll look, but they won't find you
near where they won't find me.
I will be right behind you,
knowing where not to be:

Where ends are falsely padded,
where friends turn into means.
Don't let yourself be added
to the great hill of beans.

I wasn't four or forty;
I won't be forty-six.
I don't care who's been naughty
or who's been playing tricks.

How could I, when I fidget
and laugh hysterically?
My name is not a digit.
You cannot count on me.

YOU ARE A GENIUS

I can tell you right now: this is not going to work,
so please stop convoluting. It drives me berserk.
Things have changed, you've revised, reconsidered… So what?
There are words you could say, but we both know you're not

going to say them, and, frankly, no less will suffice.
I do not plan to tell you this, no. I'll be nice,
then perform a miraculous vanishing trick,
because I am a genius and you are a dick.

Come to think of it, that's what you might want to mention
assuming you'd like to retain my attention.
Yes, those are the very words. Spit them out, quick:
'You are a genius and I am a dick.'

Or you might rather type them and send them by post,
but don't ever forget them. Remember them most.
You can utter them, butter them, spread them on toast…

(This is just the beginning, but it's a good start.)
Please imbibe them, inscribe them and learn them by heart.
They might one day inspire works of life-changing art.

I can't tell you the way. Up to you. You can pick
an amazing, gold-ink-blazing sky-writing stick,
or just launch them aloft with a buoyant high kick:
'You are a genius and I am a dick.'

JUST AS RIGHT

A year or five from now
you will forget today –
the stupid breakfast row.
You'll never laugh and say

'Remember that mad beef?
God, what a pointless spat!
I gave you so much grief,
so undeserved' – and that,

my darling one, is why
this still lives in my head,
however hard I try –
because you haven't said

anything was your bad
since you and I first met –
I can't think you'd be glad,
ever, to pay that debt.

'Remember that mad beef?
God, what a pointless spat!
You gave me so much grief,
Unjustified' – yes, that

is, hands down, what you'd say.
I'd smile; not worth the fight,
but on that future day
I would be just as right.

THIS IS GOOD NOW

The things we did and said before
are now the way-back past,
our little fling, our tiny war,
began but did not last.

This long, you think, for way-back tears
and way-back pain and rage
to dissipate? The thirteen years
until I walk on stage

and you sit in the second row
and fondly smile, and lift
your hands to clap? Our long ago
romance, our way-back rift,

mustn't be talked about again
(not that it was before).
This is Good Now; that was Bad Then.
We'll think of it no more.

Could have been four or six or nine.
Chance picked a long thirteen,
and here we are – all gone, all fine.
Better not make a scene.

A curtain call that no one chose
has pulled a fade to black.
Now learn your lines. You're 'Man who knows
that there is no way back'.

IT MATTERS

Author's note: this poem first appeared in my novel 'No One Would Do What the Lamberts Have Done'.

All of us net some wins; all suffer losses,
but something I have noticed on my journey,
a truth that I have often come across is:
it matters – whether you are an attorney,

a chiropractor, vet or idling stoner,
whatever work you do (or don't) – it matters
if you are an employee or the owner,
since formers are more vulnerable than latters.

The stoner might be poor. We might not find him
among the world's top luxury affiorders
but no firm's board has forcibly resigned him,
no one is giving him his marching orders,

the show he stars in is his own creation
for off-his-chops or worse, till clogs start popping.
His days are free from threat and subjugation.
Yes, true, he cannot go fat diamond shopping

but neither can most Type As with positions
in other people's companies. Be wiser,
IT geeks, massage therapists, opticians.
Hear this unsackable careers adviser:

no shares, no benefits and bonus package
could ever be an adequate incentive
for the precarity, the freedom lackage.
Go it alone instead, and be inventive.

Dear friend, you deserve all good things and better.
You know how much I love you and admire you.
Obey this next instruction to the letter:
never work for someone who can fire you.

TO COUNT AN ELEPHANT

The trouble with imagining
an elephant in any room
is that our minds feel free to bring
past bias to bear. Would you assume

the elephant would use its trunk
to smash a window, or to loot
your silverware, get nasty drunk
and sneer at you? Or remain mute

and, in a cruel, strategic way,
refuse eye contact (only you
are targeted, and when you say
it happened, loud 'That can't be true!'

breaks out all over)? No. My guess
is, if you're anything like me,
your mind will fill with jolly bless-
his-heart and lovely-cup-of-tea

daydreams, because unless we're thick,
oblivious or vile or mad,
the first-choice, favourite guests we'd pick?
Elephants. No, it's not a fad.

We loved the Babar books when young.
We cheered on Nelly's brave escape.
To count an elephant among
our favourite friends of curvy shape?

What joy! We picture high and wide
rooms that big ears and plump grey bellies
fit very comfortably inside –
curled up on sofas, wide-screen tellies,

all the best treats (scones, cream and jam).
This feels like useful information
if you're unwilling, as I am,
to have an awkward conversation.

BEING MEAN ON HOLIDAY

Being mean on holiday
is worse than being mean at home.
You've flown or driven all that way,
you're in Mallorca, Crete or Rome,

you've forked out all that cash. Of course
it's worse. Not my fault; not my rules.
Yes, being mean in the Azores
is worse than being mean in schools

or offices or pubs or shops.
Bad Karma comes for anyone
who jibes or agitates or stops
those *en vacances* from having fun.

And worst of all (like, you should do
penance until the end of days)
is starting on the person who
has brought you here and always pays.

GENUINE QUESTION

Author's note: a version of this poem first appeared in my most recent Poirot novel, 'The Last Death of the Year'.

It was cheating that made me hate cheating.
It was gambling that taught me to save.
Ask me how I know sin's self-defeating.
Oh, my friends: I was flawed. I was brave.

It was lying that made me hate lying.
When I faked my own death in my youth,
it was failing that led me to trying
a more promising tactic: the truth.

When you say, 'Never stray. It won't serve you,'
and advise me that sin leaves a scar
on the skin of the soul, I unnerve you
with my 'Right – but you can't know you are.'

'Well, of course that's your take. How convenient,'
you respond. Still, though, what if it's true?
Facts are neither judgmental nor lenient.
I know more about goodness than you.

CONFLICT OF INTERESTS

Today, at an appointment with my dentist,
he revealed his own teeth. That's right – he opened
his mouth, flared his lips and flashed a full set.
If you asked him why (and don't bother, please) he would say
it was part of a demonstration of how to brush
and how not to brush. He would never admit
to resentment, or wanting to hurt me.

He had teeth all along, of course, and I should have guessed,
though he kept them well hidden. I should have jumped up
and pressed his top lip hard with my index
and middle fingers, to check.

I made it clear what I wanted and hoped for.
That's why he lied.
When a dentist utters the words 'my teeth'
it ought to mean his patients' teeth, not his.
Where, otherwise, is his sense
of ownership? What's at stake in my mouth
for a man with straight white teeth of his own?

'Ever heard the phrase "conflict
of interests"?' I asked him.
He gave me a look that suggested he'd rather
I kept my mouth shut,
and yet he's a dentist and I am his patient, and that
I told him, right there?
That's the whole problem.

THE ONLY COPY ON EARTH

Satisfied that my flawless
characters have behaved impeccably
for three hundred and fourteen pages, I type
'The End' and glow inside. They are nothing
like anyone I have known. Not once
does a single one lose her cool, smack his head
with the heel of his hand at the crassness
of others, who in any case are not crass
like real human beings.

Having done this many times, I know
what's expected of me next: I'm to put
my three hundred and fourteen pages out
to be read by people who cheat
on their spouses, drive with their mobile phones
in their hands, muffle their chakras with sugary
drinks, bellow at their tiny, quaking
children, pray to sputtering gods
who are all about rules, and all for two hundred
and fifty grand a year.
That's no longer enough.

I can't bear to put my pristine
characters through it. 'Please, spare us,' they beg.
'Not again. Everybody these days is so
detestable. How can we make it through page
after page if we don't sympathize with at least one reader?
There's no one for us, the super-rational and the wholly good,
to care a damn about. They're all ruthless
narcissists or the most inert of bores.'

So tomorrow my team arrives:
little carpenters and their pet engineers.
They will make me a wooden box frame with metal hinges –
a frame that's opaque, a box that won't open without breaking.
All I'll need then is a taste-maker with a gallery
– white, central, chic –
on the prowl for his next protégé.
He'll be someone you couldn't invent if you tried
for a million years.

Not a sliced up shark this time, nor an unmade bed.
Not a tent full of antique sex, but a book you can't see and can't read.
You can only know that it's brilliant, that it's there,
though you'll want to doubt both if you care
how you look, feel and sound; if you want your money's worth.

If the taste-maker plays his part
I'll play mine – make us rich every March on the dot.
I'll do all that I can to ensure that the terrible
people miss out. Shall we say
eight hundred grand for the only copy on earth?
I will love what I do so much if it can be this.

PRIVATE CHAT

'I need to talk to you alone,' you'd say
when there were other people at the table,
and each time I assumed, and so did they,
that the word 'need' meant that you should be able,

and I'd abandon food, wine, warmth and fun,
drive us around (your need craved exercise);
you'd ask as if by right, though you had none,
invasive questions, and demand replies

that I was quite determined to withhold.
I'd tell you pleasing lies, fend off the fight,
and my reward? Allowed in from the cold –
granted permission to resume my night.

You can no longer ask me to postpone
being myself, and if you could, I'd say,
'Sorry. As you can see, I'm not alone.
Perhaps your need could call some other day?'

DID YOU PUT ON A SHIRT?

In 2015, two scientists, Professor Tim Hunt and Dr Matt Taylor, did absolutely nothing wrong at all. One made a joke; the other wore a particular shirt while appearing on TV. Both received widespread public condemnation.

I wrote about Tim Hunt again.
I argued hard and long.
Now other women, other men,
might also need a strong
defence, and so I'm asking folks
in Harlem, Hull, Hong Kong –
have you told any harmless jokes?
Have you done nothing wrong?

Then let me leap to your defence!
Did you put on a shirt
you liked (which would make perfect sense)?
Did nobody get hurt?
Did you walk past an antelope
and grin in mild surprise,
not smack it with a stethoscope
nor rub salt in its eyes

and was your grin then misconstrued
as cause for great alarm,
and did the most enormous feud
spring from the lack of harm
you did? Have you been made to feel
that now you don't belong?
I'm not surprised. The danger's real
if you do nothing wrong.

Have you neglected, all these years,
to learn to play Mahjong?
I warn you, that will end in tears.
Did you once sing the song
Come on Eileen, or eat pea soup,
or watch the film *King Kong*?
Then welcome to that hated group:
those who did nothing wrong.

Smugly, you think, 'I won't be next.
I steal and cheat and lie.'
Just wait, though, till you send a text
saying 'No milk. Please buy!' –
That's when the haters will descend.
Trust me, it won't be long.
I urge you: save yourself, my friend:
never do nothing wrong.

FOR PHOEBE (ON HER NINETEENTH BIRTHDAY, AND AFTER A DEGREE CHANGE)

You chose Creative Writing
as part of your degree
but found it uninviting.
You liked Philosophy

but not Creative Writing.
In due course, you broke free
for options more exciting:
God, then Psychology.

Still, there is no point fighting
a little verse or three
of deft creative writing:
this birthday poem from me.

ADVICE FOR BACKSTROKE SWIMMERS

If you swim with your face pointing forward,
you will see if there's someone ahead
whom you might be about to bump into.
It's a game changer. Trust me: instead

of advancing back-first and oblivious,
with your eyes trained on where you've just
been,
you could gain, with a simple rotation,
a great view of the as-yet-unseen,

which will likely include other swimmers.
With an easy and swift sleight of arms
you could veer to the left by two inches
and avoid an assortment of harms,

or alternatively, keep on going
as you are. We'll all still be alive
by this evening. It's not like you're mowing
people down on the M25,

and it's selfish to mind – super-petty –
a long scratch from a hand's careless fling.
I am clearly a joy-killing wetty.
Oh, just carry on doing your thing.

SONGS IN THE SEA

Please imagine me saying this loudly:
at the age of not-quite-53:
it's high time I admitted, and proudly,
that I like to write songs in the sea.

Every tune goes through quite a few passes:
one hour's swimming yields two drafts, or three
and though last year the waves stole my glasses,
still, I love to write songs in the sea.

I would not write a serial killer
murder mystery while doing front crawl
nor a taut psychological thriller,
but I'm happy to answer the call

of the ocean for choruses, ditties,
soaring notes at the end of each line.
I will gladly write novels in cities,
but on Porthkidney Sands, I'd decline

(which, by now, must be hardly surprising
given what I've revealed about me.)
At Porthminster, I'd start harmonising,
since I love to write songs in the sea,

and in winter, when sands are frostbitten
at Porthmeor and Porthgwidden: new rule –
it appears songs can also be written
in the Carbis Bay Spa's heated pool.

E.A. GUEST'S *IT COULDN'T BE DONE* MEETS PHILIP LARKIN'S *MR BLEANEY*

This poem and the next one were both written for a competition in The Spectator *magazine, in which the task was to write a mash-up of two famous poems. This one didn't win, but the next one did.*

Somebody said that it couldn't be done
And he, Mr Bleaney, replied
That 'Phil Larkin would say, "Soon the worms will have fun
In our skeletal mouths, gaping wide."'
Still, he buckled right in, since to hope is no sin,
Worked with grace. If Phil irked him, he hid it.
He started to sing as he tackled the thing
That couldn't be done, and he did it.

There are thousands to tell you it cannot be done
(See: poor Bleaney's curmudgeon creator)
There are many who'll say your drab room's not the one,
Like a down-in-the-dumps snobby hater,
But just buckle right in with a bit of a grin.
(Room looked *fine* when glum Phil came to view it!)
Just start in to sing as you tackle the thing
That cannot be done, and you'll do it.

EDNA ST VINCENT MILLAY'S *I, BEING BORN A WOMAN* MEETS WILLIAM CARLOS WILLIAMS'S *THE RED WHEELBARROW*

I, being born with talent, and distressed
By all the red wheelbarrows of your kind,
Have lied, pretended, still pretend, to find
Your poems bold and vibrant, well expressed.
Though, actually, your so-called verse, designed
To make a proper poet lose her mind,
Does, I'm afraid, in all ways, fail my test.
Yet how I fancy you. Oh, the poor treason
Of my stout blood against my staggering brain!
Spring, summer, fall… I shall spend each new season
Making excuses for you. All in vain.
I find your six-pack insufficient reason
For rhyme-less farm equipment in the rain.

THE MYSTERY OF MR E

A murder mystery musical

Book, all lyrics and some tunes by Sophie Hannah
Music by Annette Armitage

This musical was performed by the pupils of Sancton Wood School in Cambridge in 2017, directed by Sarah Cowen, and by the pupils of St Michael's Catholic School in Watford in 2019, directed by Laura Turner. Scene Zero Theatre Company also did a touring production (for which the title was changed to The Generalist) *with a cast comprising adults and children, for three literary festivals in 2018: Noirwich in Norwich, Bloody Scotland in Stirling, and the Cambridge Literary Festival. The musical was then made into a movie, directed by Martyn Tott, in 2023. The movie is available to watch on Amazon Prime and Apple TV and is a slightly different version from this one, which is the original stage version.*

JOHN DANES ('THE GENERALIST')
Unable to find one regular job that interests him, John has set up as a 'Generalist' – a profession he invented himself in order to earn money without getting bored.

MR E
A mysterious visitor to John's house

THE LANDRIGAN FAMILY AND HOUSEHOLD

HARRIET LANDRIGAN (deceased)
World-famous and billion-copy-selling romantic novelist. Harriet was born in 1941 and died in 2004.

PETER LANDRIGAN
Harriet's son, guardian of her legacy and manager of her literary estate's business affairs

CLEMENCY LANDRIGAN
Peter's wife, a perfume designer

OSCAR LANDRIGAN
Peter and Clemency Landrigan's 14-year-old son.

'ANDERS' (ANDREW ANDERSON)
Director of Operations at Idlewyld House. Looks after the personal and business affairs of the Landrigan family. A sort of modern-day butler, he always carries a large set of keys around with him – keys to the various doors of the house.

The Landrigans live in Idlewyld House – a large country mansion with extensive grounds. This was Harriet Landrigan's famous former home, as well as where she died, and her fans are obsessed with it.

DEVAUX 'DEEVO' RUSSELL (deceased)
Died in 2003, but before that he was Harriet Landrigan's publisher since the start of her career. He founded the publishing house Russell & Russell. Later in his career, he also wrote thrillers.

HOUSE GUESTS AT IDLEWYLD HOUSE

MAX RUSSELL
Deevo Russell's (deceased) eldest son, who now runs Russell, Russell & Russell (formerly Russell & Russell, but now with one more family member on board)

IRENE COGGINS
A Harriet Landrigan 'superfan', Irene lives and breathes Harriet Landrigan. She owns every edition of each of Harriet's books and has turned her home into a Harriet Landrigan shrine.

SWITHUN KIRK
An actor who wants to buy the film rights to one of Harriet Landrigan's novels

PROFESSOR LAURA TAYLOR
An academic who is studying Harriet Landrigan as part of a research project

TESS YOLLAND
A fine art dealer

PFFISHAM SCHOOL STAFF, PUPILS, AND PUPILS' RELATIVES

(Pffisham is pronounced Fish-um, and former pupils are 'Pffishamians'.)

MR FRIEND
Headmaster of Pffisham School, the school attended by Oscar Landrigan

BARTIE (BARTHOLOMEW) VOSS
Pffisham school's star pupil. He is 14, and in Oscar's class.

FRANK VOSS
Bartie's dad

PAMOLYN (PAM) VOSS
Bartie's mum

MRS GWEN LAPP
French teacher at Pffisham School

MISS NEARY
Music teacher at Pffisham School

MR MORRISON
History teacher at Pffisham School

'ASBO' (TOBIAS BOLAND)
Oscar's best friend at school. He and Oscar are in a gang called 'The Reprobates'

CORNELIA VAN ZUYLEN
Bartie Voss's best friend/groupie at school

3-STRIKE and FONDER
The two other members of Oscar and ASBO's reprobate gang

THE POLICE

INSPECTOR COODE
SERGEANT WILDERSPIN

WOMEN AT POLICE STATION: a group of women who make a habit of falling in love with famous murderers, all currently obsessed with Mr E

SONGS/MUSICAL NUMBERS

Overture
A Generalist Like Me
Books on a Wall
Thanks to Frank and Pam
Reconstruction
I'll Stick With Mr Friend
Peter's Lament
Greatest Fan
Clue-mont!
I'd Much Prefer to Solve a Mystery
Please Find Enclosed
Something Wrong
No Happy Ending
The Pffishamian Song (Gates of Gold)

ACT ONE

Overture starts…

SCENE 1

Interior of JOHN DANES' house. As the Overture plays, JOHN is packing a suitcase. Once it's packed, he reaches for his hat and coat. He puts them on, checks the mirror, adjusts both hat and coat, then smiles at himself. He is about to leave when there's a knock at the door.

JOHN: (*without turning to look in the direction of the door*) It's open!

Enter MR E

JOHN: (*turning*) Oh… Hello! I'm afraid I'm just leaving.

MR E: Off to Idlewyld House, are you?

JOHN: Yes, as a matter of fact. I'm sorry, who are you? We don't know each other, do we?

MR E: Not yet.

JOHN: Then how do you know I'm going to Idlewyld House? Have they sent you to collect me? I told them I'd drive.

MR E: Nobody has sent me.

JOHN: I see. Then…do you mind if I ask why you're here? And once you've told me, I must go. I don't want to be late.

MR E: (*superior, leisurely tone*) You have it all planned out, don't you?

JOHN: My schedule for the day? Yes, I do. Is there something wrong with that?

MR E: It leaves no room for the unexpected.

JOHN: Look, who are you? I'm sorry to be blunt, but I need to leave.

MR E: Who am I? That's what I came here to tell you. (*He walks to the front of the stage*) I'm the murderer.

JOHN: I beg your pardon?

MR E: I'm the murderer.

JOHN: (*laughs*) The murderer? Is this a joke? Whom have you murdered?

MR E: Have you ever solved a murder? I've heard you do all sorts of unusual jobs for all kinds of strange people. You're something of a…generalist?

JOHN: That's what it says on my business card. (*He produces this from his pocket and holds it up for MR E to read.*) 'John Danes, Generalist'.

MR E: I wouldn't have thought one could make a career out of something so vague, but I've asked around and everybody says you're very good. Good at what, though? Surely no one can be good at everything.

JOHN: Well, I'm certainly not. I'm hopeless at the things other people are good at. And you've clearly got the wrong end of the stick…

SONG NO. 1: A GENERALIST LIKE ME

JOHN sings:

You misunderstand the nature
Of the Generalist's remit.
Doing everything is not the point at all.
My career path's nomenclature
Is misleading, I'll admit –
I'd be no one in the world's first port of call.

If your kitchen taps are leaking
Then a plumber's who you'll ring
From a public place, without a fear or qualm.
If you can't hear people speaking
Even when you're listening,
Have a nurse syringe your ears – works like a charm!

For an ordinary issue
You can find a specialist
But for problems more embarrassing or weird,
Once you've wept through every tissue
You'll remember I exist
And be mighty glad the Generalist appeared.

Be it summer, be it winter, see your doctor for a splinter,
See your dentist for a toothache or a brace.
See an expert dietician if nutrition is your mission
Or an astronaut to fly to outer space.
Be it spring or be it autumn, you'll remember where you bought 'em
And you'll know how to return those shoes you've realised you hate,

But when you think 'Who's this task for?', something you're
too scared to ask for,
When it's neither this nor that and you don't want to trust to
fate…

Well, at that point I can offer you a most attractive rate
To remove the most baroque of complications from your plate.
If you're in two minds and need a third one to adjudicate,
Well, in that event, the Generalist's your mate.

There are chaps like you, quite willing
To do high-risk things like killing,
But imagine if you did it nine to five for rubbish pay –
You'd be evil, you'd be scary
And you'd have no chance to vary
Your portfolio – just murder, murder every single day.

If you'd like a new excursion,
An adventure, a diversion
You should think of being a generalist, a generalist like me.
Though in light of what's arisen,
I've a hefty hunch that prison
Is where you'll end up in due course and where you deserve to
be…

MR E: I doubt you've ever solved a murder (*thoughtfully, observing JOHN*) – yet I can see that you'd like to. You want to catch me, don't you? Well, you'd better prepare yourself for disappointment. We're going to do things the other way round. I came here to catch you.

JOHN: Catch me? That makes no sense. I'm not a criminal.

MR E: Oh, there are many ways to catch a person: in the net of an obsession, for instance. An obsession with a puzzle that can never be solved.

JOHN: (*impatient*) I've had enough of this. Nothing in the letter I received says anything about a murder. (*He pulls a folded letter out of his pocket, unfolds it and starts to read it aloud.*) 'Dear Mr Danes, please arrive at Idlewyld House on the 24th of November at four o'clock. You will be received by Peter Landrigan, son of the late Harriet Landrigan. As you might know, Harriet Landrigan is the bestselling romantic novelist of all time. Indeed, she is almost the bestselling *novelist* of all time. Some say she invented the love story as we know it. She is outsold only by the Bible, Shakespeare and Agatha Christie. As the guardian of Harriet's estate and legacy, Peter Landrigan has a proposal he wishes to put to you. He greatly looks forward to meeting you….' Etcetera. (*He stuffs the letter back into his pocket*) No mention of a murder!

MR E: That doesn't surprise me.

JOHN: Listen, I've had enough of your cryptic nonsense. Tell me your name or leave at once.

MR E: Why don't I do both? (*He produces a card from his pocket, drops it on the floor, then leaves.*)

JOHN: (*walks over, picks up the card*) "Mr E". No address, no phone number… (*Calls after him*) Wait. Mr E! Come back and explain yourself! (*Hurrying, hoping to catch him, he follows MR E offstage.*)

******

SCENE 2

Flashback scene. Set and lighting should indicate that we're in the past. Enter HARRIET LANDRIGAN and DEEVO RUSSELL. HARRIET walks to the front corner of the stage carrying a book and a letter. The book is The Heaviest Heart, *one of her own novels. DEEVO walks to the other front corner of the stage. He's holding two letters. HARRIET opens her book and begins to read aloud to the audience…*

HARRIET: 'This book is dedicated to my devoted fans all over the world. It is the last book I will publish, though not the last book I shall write. I wish things could be different, but they are not.'

DEEVO: (*reading his letter aloud to the audience*) 'Dearest Harriet, I have returned from seemingly endless meetings in New York to find a finished copy of *The Heaviest Heart* on my desk. It's your best novel yet without a doubt. It's also an object of great beauty, but its dedication – which I must admit I failed to notice at the copy-edit stage, incompetent publisher that I am… Its dedication, Harriet, is most alarming. Why on earth should you wish to stop publishing your books? Unless I've misunderstood, you're saying that you intend to *write* more novels, but not publish them. Please assure me without delay that this is some sort of joke. Yours devotedly, Deevo.'

HARRIET: (*closes book and now reads from letter*) 'Dear Deevo, It is no joke. And now, I imagine, you will batter away at my defences until I have no choice but to explain myself to you, so let me say emphatically that I do not wish to explain – not to you, nor to anybody else. Yours, Harriet.'

DEEVO: (*reads from second letter*) 'Dearest Harriet, I demand to know the background to this calamitous decision. The world – and most of all, I – cannot survive without your wonderful love stories. Also, I had better warn you that when I receive your explanation I shall not accept it. Yours, dejected, baffled and determined to change your mind, Deevo.'

SCENE 3

Idlewyld House Entrance Hall. ANDERS opens the door to JOHN DANES. ANDERS carries a large bunch of keys (he always has these with him – in every scene, he's holding them.)

ANDERS: (*ushering JOHN inside*) You must be John Danes. Welcome to Idlewyld House. I'm Andrew Anderson, Director of Operations here. Everyone calls me Anders, and you must do the same.

JOHN: Thank you. (*JOHN puts his suitcase down somewhere out of the way.*) Sorry I'm late. I got lost in the grounds. There's another large building…

ANDERS: Yes, I can see it would be confusing. That's Pffisham School. Your host, Peter Landrigan, has also been delayed, and in that very building. (*In a weary and knowing tone*) It's prize-giving day. Oscar, Peter's fourteen-year-old son, won't have won anything. He never does. Which means that Clemency, Peter's wife, will at this moment be berating the poor headmaster, as she *always* does.

JOHN: (*laughs*) Oh dear! (*He takes off his hat and coat and hands them to ANDERS, who hangs them up.*)

ANDERS: Yes. I'm afraid that, until the school creates a prize for 'Pupil With The Most Under-Employed Brain Cells', Oscar won't be winning any awards. Don't tell Clemency I said that, or I'll lose my job.

JOHN: (*a little startled to be so confided in*) I see.

ANDERS: Laziness – that's Oscar's problem. Beyond the basics of eating and breathing, he's unwilling to exert himself. I call it 'The Idlewyld Curse'. I've told Peter and Clemency, but they won't listen. Until they change the name of this house, every child born here will be either idle or wild. Peter was wild in his youth. As was his mother, the late, great Harriet. Wildness can be harnessed and channelled into a powerful creative force, whereas the idle – like young Oscar – rarely achieve anything.

JOHN: I don't think you should assume the poor boy's doomed to failure if he's only fourteen.

ANDERS: Don't you? You will once you've met him.

JOHN: I don't believe in curses, either. Or anything else that's scientifically impossible.

ANDERS: (*looks wise – as if he knows better*) There's a boy in Oscar's year called Bartholomew Voss. Bartie. He wins the school's outstanding achievement prize every time it's awarded. His address? *Number one* Bedwell Gardens. I suppose you'd say that's a coincidence?

JOHN: (*giving him a strange look*) Do you mind if I ask you something? You seem…indiscreet, so perhaps you'll give me an honest answer. Has there been a murder here?

ANDERS: That's an interesting question. In the letter of invitation you received, did it say that there had been a murder?

JOHN: No.

ANDERS: Then where did you get the idea from?

JOHN: *Has* there been a murder?

ANDERS: Officially? No. But I've never been sure, myself.

JOHN: That's a strange thing to say.

ANDERS: Let me show you something, before the family returns. Follow me.

They exit.

SCENE 4

Idlewyld House Drawing Room. On a wall are four framed books. All are leather bound and the author's name on each one, embossed in gold, is 'Harriet Landrigan'. HARRIET enters. We understand immediately that she's not alive, but, rather, is a ghostly presence in her former home. She steps forward to the front of the stage and starts to sing, while looking at/ gesturing towards the books, to draw the audience's attention to them.

SONG NO. 2: BOOKS ON A WALL

HARRIET sings:

Follow him, follow me
To the books on a wall,
Little worlds behind glass
That make no sense at all.

There's a word in a line,
There's a line on a page,
There's a page in a book
And the book's on a stage,

And a man stands and stares
In a play, in a hall,
Who'll one day tell a story of books on a wall.

(Enter JOHN and ANDERS, while HARRIET is singing. They don't see or feel her ghostly presence, but they walk over to the books. JOHN inspects them with great interest.)

There's a scene in a room
Where a woman will laugh.
There's a twist hidden deep
In a long paragraph;

There's a chance at the end,
There's no hope at the start,
Just a tear in an eye
And a tear in a heart,

And a man stands and looks
And sees nothing at all
In a search for a story of books on a wall.

Follow him, follow me
To the books on the wall,
Little worlds behind glass
That make no sense at all.

Exit HARRIET

JOHN: (*sounding increasingly puzzled as he reads the four books' titles, embossed in gold on their covers)*

'The Man She Thought She Knew'
'She Loved A Liar'
'The Love That You Deserve'
'A Bond Betrayed'

(*He turns to face ANDERS, puzzled.*) All by Harriet Landrigan. I don't understand. What *are* these?

Lights go down.

******

SCENE 5

Pffisham School hall. Present are: Headmaster MR FRIEND, FRANK and PAMOLYN VOSS, BARTIE VOSS, PETER LANDRIGAN, CLEMENCY LANDRIGAN, OSCAR LANDRIGAN, GWEN LAPP, MISS NEARY, MR MORRISON, CORNELIA VAN ZUYLEN, ASBO, FONDER, 3-STRIKE, OTHER PARENTS AND CHILDREN AND TEACHERS

MR FRIEND is standing centre-stage.

MR FRIEND: And once again, the Outstanding Achievement Award goes to… Bartholomew Voss!

Loud cheering from everyone, but especially from FRANK and PAMOLYN VOSS. CLEMENCY LANDRIGAN does not clap or cheer. BARTIE VOSS stands up and walks over to MR FRIEND, bowing to everyone and grinning charmingly. He shakes MR FRIEND's hand and accepts his award.

BARTIE: Thank you very much, sir. And please…do call me Bartie.

PAMOLYN VOSS and FRANK VOSS stand up. PAMOLYN points a camera at BARTIE.

PAMOLYN: Smile, darling, for Mummy's photo!

CLEM: That infuriating Voss boy wins every time, Peter! Why don't they just give him a 'Forever the Best' prize and spare us the ordeal of slogging all the way over here to receive the utterly predictable news that he's won yet again?

PETER: 'All the way over here'? Darling, the school's in our garden.

CLEM: Yes it is – and if Oscar doesn't win the award next time, I shall dig up the whole wretched institution and toss it in the compost!

PETER: (*seeing that BARTIE's about to speak*): Ssh!

BARTIE: Thank you. Thank you all so much. (*Clears throat.*) Success and excellence are never the achievements of only one person. I would be neither so successful nor so excellent without Mr Friend and the superb teachers of Pffisham School, and I'm hugely grateful to you all…

PAMOLYN: (*steps forward to attract BARTIE's attention, pointing at herself*) But most of all, last but not least…

FRANK: (*stands up, shouts*) Stand up straight, Bartholomew! Project your voice! And remember, you can win every prize going and still be Not Quite Good Enough! (*This last line is delivered not snidely but as if it's a great and helpful piece of advice that BARTIE will appreciate.*)

BARTIE: (*straightens his back, projects his voice more*) But I am even more grateful to the two most important people in my life (*he gestures towards PAMOLYN and FRANK*): my guiding lights, Mum and Dad – both of whom are Old Pffishamians, of course. In my opinion, children should praise their parents in front of an audience far more often than they do. And so I'd like to share with everybody here today my special words of thanks for two magnificent human beings, Pamolyn and Frank Voss.

Applause breaks out.

SONG NO. 3: THANKS TO FRANK AND PAM

BARTIE sings:

It's such a treat to have the chance to say how proud I am
To be the son of Dad and Mum (whom you will know as Frank and Pam).
I could praise them for a thousand years and still not overstate
Their devoted contribution to me ending up so great.

If I'm soon to have, as I surely am, many billions in the bank,
I'll have got that far thanks to Ma and Pa. (You can call them Pam and Frank.)
It was clear as day from when I was one and I built my own first pram
What a brilliant life that had just begun, and it's thanks to Frank and Pam.

Because success is all that matters – concrete proof you've passed the test.
Any old child can gawp at YouTube and then say 'I tried my best.'
Do not tell your son you love him if he's not a high achiever.
He'll retire to bed immediately with can't-be-bothered fever.

If I'm soon to have, as I surely am, many billions in the bank,
I'll have got that far thanks to Ma and Pa. (You can call them Pam and Frank.)

CORNELIA sings:

It was clear as day from when he was one and he built his own first pram
What a brilliant life that had just begun, and it's thanks to Frank and Pam.

BARTIE sings:

So don't pretend that kindness counts for more than global domination.
Your child might end up flogging lattes from a hatch at Cambridge station.
Never tell him bedtime stories – that will only keep him needing.
Throw the works of Henry James into his cot and yell, 'Start reading!'

BARTIE and CORNELIA sing:

If I'm soon to have (If he's soon to have)
As I surely am (As he surely is)
Many billions in the bank,
I'll have got that far (He'll have got that far)
Thanks to Ma and Pa. (Thanks to Ma and Pa.)
You can call them Pam and Frank.
It was clear as day, from when I/he was one, and I/he built my/his own first pram
What a brilliant life that had just begun, and it's thanks to Frank and Pam.

Everywhere I go (Everywhere he goes)
Everyone will know (As the legend grows)
What a superstar I am,
I'll have got that far (He'll have got that far)
Thanks to Ma and Pa, (Thanks to Ma and Pa,)
So hurrah for Frank and Pam,
So hurrah for Frank and Pam,
So hurrah for Frank! And! Pam!

After the song is clearly finished, FRANK and PAMOLYN want it to continue, so they start to sing in praise of themselves:

FRANK: So hurrah for Frank and Pam! Come on, everybody, join in!

PAMOLYN: Huge hurrahs for Frank and Pa-am! They're the best, are Frank and Pa–am…

CLEM: I can't bear much more of this. Come on, Peter. And you, Oscar. We're leaving.

PETER and OSCAR exit. CLEMENCY is intercepted by MR FRIEND on her way out.

MR FRIEND: I hope you've had an enjoyable afternoon, Mrs Landrigan?

CLEM: I have *not,* Mr Friend. You're going to have to expel Bartie Voss. I've been lenient until now, but there's simply no other way.

MR FRIEND: Expel him? But he's our best…

CLEM: Do not argue with me! Having a child here who does so well creates the impression that the teachers are good – which is highly misleading. You need to start firing people –- the French teacher especially. Mrs Lapp. She's *hopeless.* All the French Oscar knows, he's learned from me*:* Yves St Laurent, Thierry Mugler… And if I didn't happen to be a perfume designer, he wouldn't even know that much!

MR FRIEND: Mrs Landrigan…

CLEM: (*holds up a hand to silence him*) Also. Oscar finds his walk to school intolerably tiring…

MR FRIEND: Oh, no, not this again. Mrs Landrigan, be reasonable. We've already moved the school into your garden because you refused to drive across town. We can't move it again.

CLEM: Yes, you can, and you will. If this school is not at least two hundred yards closer to my house by this time next week, there will be consequences. Do you hear me, Mr Friend? *Consee-Quences.* (*She sighs*) I'll have Anders move the old stables. The school can go there. That will be close enough, I expect. And if it isn't, we can think about relocating you again. To my conservatory.

MR FRIEND: (*turns away*) Oh, God, kill me now.

CLEM: Though it'll have to wait until I've launched my new fragrance. (*She fans herself with her hands.)* I'm *extremely* stressed and overwhelmed at the moment. (*She sweeps out of the room and exits.*)

MR FRIEND: (*sarcastically*) Can't imagine how that feels. (*Exits on the other side of the stage*)

SCENE 6

Idlewyld House Drawing Room. ANDERS and JOHN are still looking at the wall, at the glass-fronted wooden box frames with HARRIET's books inside them.

JOHN: Well, are you going to tell me or not? (*Gestures towards the framed books on the wall.*) What are they?

ANDERS: What do they look like?

JOHN: Books. Except…they're framed. Stuck behind glass and mounted on the wall. *Are* they books? Or are they works of art?

ANDERS: In a way, they're both. Let me explain…

Enter PETER LANDRIGAN

PETER: Perhaps I should be the one to explain. Hello, Mr Danes. Good to meet you. I'm Peter Landrigan.

JOHN: Please, call me John. (*The two of them shake hands.*)

PETER: Do sit down.

JOHN pulls over a chair and sits.

PETER: I assume you've heard of my mother – Harriet Landrigan? She died in 2004, at the age of only 63. Far too young. You will know, I'm sure, that her love stories have sold in their billions.

JOHN: Indeed! Who hasn't heard of Harriet Landrigan?

PETER: She's outsold only by the Bible, Agatha Christie and… (*frustrated to have forgotten*) Anders, who's the other one?

ANDERS: (*trying and failing to conceal his contempt.*) William Shakespeare is *the other one.*

PETER: (*looking pleased to have solved the problem*) That's the chap! May I ask you, John…do you know anything else about my mother? Are you aware of the mystery that surrounds her life and work?

JOHN: No, I don't think so.

PETER: Well, I'll tell you – though I should say, it has nothing to do with why I've invited you here. But since Anders has shown you the framed books… At a certain point in her career – 1998, if you're interested in the exact date – my mother stopped publishing her novels. She continued to write them, and worked as hard on them as she always had, but nothing anyone said or did could persuade her to publish them. Not the sacks full of begging letters from her fans, nor the offers of more money from her publisher. She refused point blank. Instead, she hand-wrote each novel in a large, leather-bound notebook, and had it framed. 'You may hang them on the walls as if they were works of art, Peter,' she told me. 'But that is all. They are never to leave Idlewyld House, never to be sold and never to be read by anybody.'

JOHN: How extraordinary.

ANDERS: Isn't it just?

JOHN: Why bother writing novels that she didn't want anyone to read?

PETER: I've really no idea.

ANDERS: No one knows why she did it. Harriet refused to explain.

PETER: It's a terribly sad story, as well as a mystery. You see, Mother's books were always published by DeVaux Russell, right from the start. I trust you've heard of him?

JOHN: I'm afraid not.

PETER: What? You've never heard of DeVaux Russell? He was *the* great publisher of the twentieth century! Wrote a couple of books himself, too, as a sideline – rather violent thrillers, I believe. Deevo, Mother used to call him. He founded the publishing house Russell & Russell. Thanks to the Harriet Landrigan books, his company was immensely profitable…

ANDERS: …until Harriet announced that she would never again publish another novel. Deevo's firm soon went bankrupt without her contribution to its annual profits. Deevo took up first drinking, then gambling…(*sighs*) Then skateboarding…then spray-painting graffiti onto the walls of other publishers' office buildings. He eventually died of liver failure.

JOHN: How appalling.

PETER: There's a sort of silver lining. Deevo's two sons and his nephew restarted the business after his death. Russell & Russell is once again a thriving publishing company, except now it's called…oh, blast, I always forget the name! What's it called now, Anders?

ANDERS: (*sighs*) It's called Russell, *Russell* & Russell.

PETER: Indeed! Russell, *Russell* & Russell. They still publish my mother's novels …(*he points to the wall*) …though obviously not all of them.

JOHN: (*approaches the framed books on the wall*) Deevo must have wished he could get his hands on these unpublished ones.

PETER: Absolutely. It would have saved his business.

ANDERS: Not to mention his life.

JOHN: (*looking closely at the framed books*) Now that Harriet's dead, aren't you tempted to smash the glass and see what's in these books? I'd be keen to know what she was so determined nobody should read. You could even publish them, assuming the contents weren't too controversial.

PETER: Of course I'm tempted. But I won't do it because it would be against my mother's clearly stated wishes. Couldn't live with myself, I'm afraid.

JOHN: When did Deevo Russell die? Before or after Harriet?

PETER: One year before her – almost to the day. My mother died on the twenty-first of July 2004. Deevo died on the nineteenth of July 2003.

JOHN: If you don't mind my asking, how did Harriet die?

Enter MR E. The other characters don't notice him. They silently move and mouth words while he speaks, to indicate that they're still chatting and unaware of his presence. He walks to the front of the stage and talks directly to the audience:

MR E He's a sharp one, this John Danes. I could give him the answer, but I won't.

PETER: (*to JOHN*) My mother's death was a tragic accident. She fell down the stairs and broke her neck – here, at Idlewyld House. The doctors did all they could to save her life. I subsequently donated a significant amount of money to the hospital, to show how grateful I was for their efforts. Sadly, those efforts were in vain.

MR E: (*to audience*) It wasn't a tragic accident. It was murder. That ought to have been obvious, but people are so unimaginative. I'm surprised any crimes ever get solved. DNA testing, digital this-and-that – all these technological advances are no substitute for logic and intuition. And don't get me started on scene-of-crime reconstructions…

PETER, JOHN and ANDERS sit or stand very still, as if frozen, while MR E walks slowly around them.

SONG NO. 4: RECONSTRUCTION

MR E sings:

Most of the witnesses insist
The room is as it was before.
They do their best, but they persist
In seeing only what they saw
And missing what they've always missed.

They shut their eyes. They walk around
But nothing seems to spring to mind.
How will they know when they have found
Whatever they're supposed to find?
Is it a smell? Is it a sound?

They do not know and cannot guess
What might be meant by evidence.
Since none of them would dare confess
Their presence here makes little sense
But they are happy more or less

With things exactly as they are.
The first impression is the last.
The truth, it lies too far away for them to reach.
The past is like a disappearing star.
The past is like a disappearing star;
The past… is like… a disappearing star.

Lights go down.

SCENE 7

Idlewyld House Drawing Room. PETER, JOHN and ANDERS are already there. Enter CLEMENCY LANDRIGAN.

CLEM: (*charming and jolly, very different from how she was at the school*) Oh – hello! You must be John Danes, the Generalist. How lovely to meet you! Tell me, what exactly *is* a generalist? I've never heard of the profession before.

JOHN: It's not a profession. It's just me. I'm the only one.

CLEM: How terribly exciting! I do so love a truly unique person. My son Oscar is unique. You must meet him. (*Bellows*) Oscar!!

ANDERS rolls his eyes.

PETER: John, forgive me, but…if you're the only one, then where does the job title 'Generalist' come from? And what does it mean? I hired you because a good friend of mine told me you'd helped him greatly, but I must confess, I'm not at all sure what you do.

JOHN: I made up the job title. Had to call myself something, didn't I? As for what I do…well, I do all kinds of things. I do…general stuff, whatever people want me to do.

CLEM: Oh, how marvellous! General stuff! You don't want an apprentice, do you? I'm sure Oscar could do general stuff. Don't you think so, Anders?

ANDERS: (*carefully*) I expect Oscar would be as adept at the general as he is at the specific.

CLEM: (*proudly, misunderstanding him*) He certainly would!

PETER: Could you tell us about some of the…uh…general stuff you've done, John?

JOHN: Gladly. One of my favourites was the woman who paid me a huge amount of money to hire a series of cars – a different one every week – and park them next to a particular stretch of pavement on her street. All I had to do was leave each car in the designated spot for a week, then go and pick it up and return it to the car hire place.

CLEM: Why on earth did she want you to do that?

JOHN: Revenge. On a vindictive neighbour. For some reason, he believed that bit of road was his own personal parking space – which it definitely wasn't. It was a public street, no yellow lines or anything. Anyone was allowed to park there. But her neighbour had no garage or driveway of his own, no off-road parking of any kind and…well, clearly he was bitter about it. One day my client parked her car on the stretch of road just next to his house, which he unreasonably thought of as his, and when she returned to it a couple of hours later, she caught him vandalising it – can of spray paint in hand and everything!

CLEM: Why didn't she go straight to the police?

JOHN: She did. The neighbour denied it, and it was his word against hers. The police said nothing more could be done. My client disagreed – which led to her becoming…my client.

CLEM: Did the neighbour vandalise any of the cars you left in 'his' so-called parking space?

JOHN: Nope. But apparently he stood in his front garden and stared at them for hours on end, and one occasion, my client saw him crying.

PETER: How extraordinary. (*Shaking his head*) The daft things people find to get upset about…

CLEM: Do tell us another, John. It's so fascinating.

JOHN: They're not all as bizarre as the car parking one. Last week, I helped a widow decide what breed of dog would suit her best. Her husband had died and she wanted a puppy, to keep her company. She couldn't make a decision on her own – her husband had made all the decisions for both of them for forty years. I told her to get an Old English Sheepdog. She took my advice, and now she and her new dog are very happy together.

PETER: I don't think I'd like to be a generalist. It sounds rather… unpredictable.

JOHN: Oh, it is! Next week I'm being paid to attend a course in Basingstoke called 'Heal Your Inner Child'. I'll have to hold hands with strangers and weep in public, all because my client – the one whose inner child needs healing, according to him – is too shy to do it himself. He's paying me for a detailed report of the whole shebang, after which he hopes to be able to heal *his* inner child in the privacy of his own home.

CLEM: That's *such* an inspiring story! Mr Danes –

JOHN: Do call me John.

CLEM: John…would you mind if I created a fragrance for men and called it 'The Generalist'? I hope my husband mentioned in his letter that I'm a perfume designer?

PETER: John, why did you ask how my mother died?

JOHN: Hm? Oh. Well, yes, I suppose I should tell you. A rather extraordinary thing happened just before I set off to come here. A man I'd never met before – a complete stranger – turned up at my house and told me that he was 'the murderer'. Of whom, he did not say. Nor would he tell me his name, though he left his card which had a sort of name on it – 'Mr E' – and nothing apart from that, no contact details. Somehow, he knew that I was on my way to Idlewyld House.

ANDERS: And you assumed this chap was talking about a murder that had happened here?

JOHN: Yes. I thought maybe you'd asked me here in the hope that I could solve it.

PETER: No. There has been no murder here. How peculiar. Ah well, it must have been a practical joke of some sort. I'd forget all about it if I were you.

CLEM: Don't be an idiot, Peter. Who could forget something like that? It sounds rather significant to me – definitely worth remembering.

JOHN: May I ask, Mr Landrigan…why *did* you summon me here? What is it that you want me to do?

PETER: Yes, let me explain.

(from offstage, OSCAR yells, 'Anders, I'm hungry! Can you make me a sandwich?')

PETER: (*glances to where the noise came from*) Wait – here comes Oscar, with our other guests in tow.

JOHN: Other guests? Oh! I didn't realise…

PETER: Perhaps we should step into the library for a moment, so that we can talk in private. Come this way (*he gestures towards the door*)…

PETER and JOHN exit.

Enter OSCAR holding a bit of paper with writing on it – he approaches CLEMENCY. Following after him are IRENE COGGINS, PROFESSOR LAURA TAYLOR, SWITHUN KIRK, TESS YOLLAND and MAX RUSSELL.

OSCAR: (*hands the paper to CLEMENCY*) Mum, I've got French homework and I don't understand it.

CLEM: Oh, damn and blast the infernal Mrs Lapp! Darling, Mummy has a new fragrance to design *and* a house full of guests. She doesn't have time for French homework – especially not when it's been set by that appalling Lapp woman.

OSCAR: Well, I can't do it on my own. And if I don't do it, I'll get another warning.

CLEM: (*Dejected*) Oh! (*Perks up*) I know! Go and hide it in a book in the library. We'll say Mrs Lapp never gave it to you. You never saw it. I never saw it. Our guests never saw it. No one will be able to prove it ever existed.

OSCAR: Can't Anders hide it for me?

CLEM: Oscar! What sort of attitude is that?

OSCAR: (*sulkily*) All *right*. I'll do it myself.

(*OSCAR exits.*)

PROFESSOR LAURA TAYLOR approaches CLEM and clears her throat.

PROF T: I couldn't help overhearing… I know I'm bound to say this, as a university professor, but isn't it rather irresponsible to tell your son to hide his homework and deny all knowledge of it?

CLEM: It would be, yes, if he had a French teacher who played fair. Instead, he has Gwen Lapp who, believe me, deserves everything she gets, *and* all the homework she *doesn't* get.

The other guests walk over and join in the conversation.

MAX: Come now, surely she can't be that bad?

SWITHUN: Why not? Some people are. Try being an actor if you don't believe me. After I won my first Oscar, I had the misfortune to work with the most appalling director. He–

TESS: Come off it! You actors have it easy compared to us suckers in the art world. You should try dealing with tortured genius artists.

MAX: I suppose you're all waiting for me to chip in as a publisher and say that authors are the worst of all?

IRENE: Don't you dare, Max! It would be an insult to the memory of the late, great Harriet Landrigan – and in her home, too.

SWITHUN: (*to TESS*) Tess, have you met Irene? She's what's known as a 'superfan' of Harriet Landrigan. Knows the books inside out, and all the personal trivia. Ask her what Harriet had for breakfast on any day of her life – she'll be able to tell you. I tried it once. 'April the 17th, 1975,' I said. Quick as a flash, Irene said… (*he takes the scarf from around Irene's neck, drapes it around his own, and imitates her voice.*) 'Easy! Sardines on toast.'

MAX: (*to IRENE*) I don't suppose you know the answer to the biggest mystery of all: why Harriet stopped publishing the books she wrote?

IRENE: (*firmly and priggishly*) No, I don't. Nor do I wish to know. If Harriet didn't want to tell us – and she plainly didn't – then it's quite right and fitting for it to remain forever a mystery.

MAX: (*to CLEM*) Can we at least solve the mystery of the dreadful French teacher, Mrs Lapp? What is so terribly wrong with her?

CLEM: You won't believe me if I tell you. It sounds too ridiculous.

ANDERS: That's because it *is* ridiculous.

CLEM: Oscar's school is a very special place. Oh, I moan about it all the time, but I love it really. Mr Friend, the headmaster, is keen to give people a chance, you see. (*She pulls a handkerchief out of her pocket and twirls it around as she speaks.*) It's a very compassionate school…

TESS: I sense there's a 'but' on the way?

CLEM: The problem is, Mr Friend extends his policy of giving second chances to the teachers as well as the pupils. And, while I approve of that in theory, when you apply it to someone like Gwen Lapp…

SWITHUN: (*taking the handkerchief from Clemency's hand and waving it in the air with a flourish)* Please don't keep us in suspense any longer. What's wrong with the woman?

CLEM: What's wrong is that she doesn't want to be a secondary school French teacher, and she makes that perfectly obvious to all her pupils. A teacher can harbour whatever hopes and dreams she chooses, of course – that's up to her – but she should hide her personal ambition from the children and get on with teaching her subject properly.

MAX: Can't argue with that. Still, it must be terribly hard to have a vocation and feel unable to pursue it.

PROF. T: And probably equally hard not to have a clue what one wants to be.

MAX: Indeed. Speaking of which, this chap John Danes – the Generalist… He's chosen an interesting line of work, hasn't he?

PROF. T: Who?

MAX: One of our fellow guests – we'll meet him any minute now, I expect. As soon as Peter told me about him, I set my heart on publishing his memoirs one day. I'm sure they'd be fascinating.

IRENE: (*to CLEM*) So what *does* Mrs Lapp want to be, if not a secondary school French teacher?

SWITHUN: A film star like me, probably. Isn't that what most people want to be?

CLEM: Nothing so straightforward, I'm afraid.

TESS: Then what? Tell us.

CLEM: She wants to be…(*heavy sigh*)…State's Attorney for Pima County, Arizona. In America.

PROF T: Goodness me. That's very specific.

CLEM: Despite having been born in Saffron Walden and spending her entire life in England, she feels it's her vocation to be a blowhard Arizona prosecutor. It's all she cares, talks or thinks about! She knows *no* French, apart from one phrase: '*Pouvez-vous verifier les pneus*?' That means, 'Can you check the tyres?' She doesn't even know how to say 'The bakery is on the left' and things like that! The absolute basics! And when Oscar makes mistakes in his homework, she writes 'Objection: hearsay' in his exercise book, or 'Objection: assumes facts not yet in evidence'. It really is intolerable! Still… No matter how much I complain I always end up reaching the same conclusion…

SONG NO. 5: I'LL STICK WITH MR FRIEND

CLEM sings:

The Pffisham School's a noble, great and worthy institution,
The headmaster, Mr Friend, is skilled at conflict resolution,
He's devoted to his pupils and he'll get them prepped for unis,
(And he'll never mention if their mums are narcissistic loonies.)
On the rare occasions when I storm in spoiling for a fight,
He says, 'Have next term for free,' and 'Mrs Landrigan, you're right.'
Still, I lie awake at night and wonder: should I cut my losses?
Can my heart withstand more Prize Days with those egomaniac Vosses?

So I make a long, long list of schools,
Then I think of all their pointless rules
That the Heads might not let me amend...
Then I thank my stars for Mr Friend.

IRENE, PROF T, MAX, TESS and SWITHUN sing:

So she makes a long, long list of schools
Then she thinks of all their pointless rules
That the Heads might not let her amend...
Then she thanks her stars for Mr Friend.

CLEM sings:

I have to say, the most unnerving problem is the teachers,
Who (I can't help thinking) ought to be among a school's best features.
If you'll listen I will tell you: it's not only Mrs Lapp.
There's a brand new history teacher who's a most peculiar chap.

He can sulk for hours if he's not met with rapturous applause,
Just because his name's Jim Morrison, like that bloke from The Doors.
And the English teacher, every break, kicks footballs at my car.
She's convinced that in a past life she was Eric Cantona.

So I make a list of schools I've heard
Do a decent job and aren't absurd,
Then I hear how much I would have to spend...
And I think I'll stick with Mr Friend.

IRENE, PROF T, MAX, TESS and SWITHUN sing:

So she makes a list of schools she's heard
Do a decent job and aren't absurd,
Then she hears how much she would have to spend...
She decides to stick with Mr Friend.

CLEM sings:

I naively thought the drama teacher quite liked teaching drama
'Til I heard her voice a fervent wish to be…the Dalai Lama,
And the cupboard that pretends to be a classroom fit for Latin
Smells as mouldy as a dustbin with the remnants of a rat in.
The canteen staff are deluded. To a man, they've lost their marbles.
They're obsessed with thefts of bread, like Javert from Les Misérables.
When the Ofsted flunkies do their checks, the staff presents as sane;
The inspectors leave, and bonkers-ness takes over once again…

So I make a list and I'm all, like, 'Yay!'
But the schools are all so far away
With a five mile drive at each day's end...
So I think I'll stick with Mr Friend.

IRENE, PROF T, TESS, SWITHUN and MAX sing:

'Cause he nods and grins and he says, 'Yeah, fine,'
Then he takes a pen and he draws a line
Through the words 'Detention this weekend'.
She is oh-so-fond of Mr Friend.

CLEM sings:

'Cause he sees my point every time I say
That the boy might do some work one day
But for now it's cool if we just pretend.
Every school should have a Mr Friend.

ALL sing:

Every school should have a Mr Friend! Frie-e-end!

Everyone exits, except ANDERS and IRENE.

IRENE: I feel most uneasy about this little gathering, Anders. All these people, poking their noses into Harriet's private business. How many of them know about the missing letters?

ANDERS: (*surprised*) Well...you do, apparently. Max, obviously. And I imagine Peter is telling Mr Danes about them at this very moment.

IRENE: I hope and pray that those letters are never found. Harriet's decision to stop publishing her books is no business of anybody's. How dare they try to get their grubby hands on all her secrets? She would have hated it! They clearly don't understand anything about what sort of person she was.

ANDERS: You do, I suppose.

IRENE: I believe so, yes.

ANDERS: Yet you fail to take into account something rather basic: it's her last four books that Harriet was determined no one should read. As far as I know, she never expressed a desire to prevent anyone from reading her letters. And the missing ones were stolen after her death. Therefore, it must have been someone else who didn't want those to come to light. Not Harriet.

IRENE: (*frowns as she realises she might be wrong about something Harriet-related. Then, furious, blustering, embarrassed at being corrected...*) Do you know what drink Harriet drank immediately before she had the terrible accident that ended up killing her?

ANDERS: No, I don't.

IRENE: (*snapping at him*) Well, I *do*. Earl Grey tea with lemon. So now you can jolly well shut up!

They exit.

SCENE 8

PETER and JOHN are in the library. There's a table with a pile of books on it. OSCAR runs in and picks up a couple of books from the pile on the table.

PETER: Oscar, we're trying to have a private conversation here.

OSCAR: Mum told me to hide my French homework in a book. S'all right, it won't take long. (*He stuffs the homework into a book and runs out again. From offstage he shouts…*) Anders! Where's my sandwich?

PETER: (*shaking his head in disappointment at his son's behaviour*) Sorry about that. Where were we?

JOHN: We were talking about Deevo Russell, your mother's publisher. You'd started to tell me about some letters.

PETER: Oh, yes. One of the guests at Idlewyld House tonight is Max Russell – Deevo's son, and managing director of the reincarnated publishing house, Russell & Russell… (*scratches head and frowns*) Though I don't think it's called that any more…

JOHN: (*tentatively, not wanting to seem as if he knows more than Peter*) No, it's now called, I think…Russell, Russell & Russell, Anders mentioned?

PETER: (*beams*) That's right! The three Russells in charge now are Deevo's two sons and his nephew. Max is one of the sons. Shortly after his father's death, he visited the firm's archive. He found that several letters between Harriet and Deevo were missing – a whole month's correspondence had vanished.

JOHN: Perhaps Harriet and Deevo didn't write to one another during that month.

PETER: They did. There was a break-in. Both Max and I have spoken to the archivist. She says the target was clearly the Harriet Landrigan material. The thief removed a number of letters. We know this because the *next* letter Harriet wrote to Deevo, after the ones that were stolen, leaves no room for doubt.

Enter HARRIET. She walks to the front of the stage.

HARRIET: (*holding letter, reads aloud*) 'Dear Deevo, (*long-ish pause. Then, sternly*) I refuse to keep going back and forth with you. For some weeks now, I have been trying to explain to you why I will never again publish another novel. If you still don't understand, then you never will. I know this is hard for you, but you will simply have to take no for an answer. My feelings matter as much as your company's profits, at least to me. I have told no one my reason apart from you. I shall leave it to you to decide whether to share it with anybody else. Regards, Harriet.'

Exit HARRIET.

JOHN: So the missing letters…

PETER: …contain my mother's explanation of why she was determined to seal her last four books behind glass so that no one could ever read them. Whoever stole those letters from the archive didn't want the truth to come to light.

JOHN: How fascinating. And you say Deevo's son Max Russell is here today?

PETER: Yes. We have several guests: Max; Professor Laura Taylor from the University of...somewhere or other, I always forget. Then we have Irene Coggins, a devoted Harriet Landrigan fan; Swithun Kirk, the actor –

JOHN: Not that talentless poser!

PETER: I'm afraid so. And a fine art dealer called Tess Yolland. You'll meet them all soon enough.

JOHN: Would you mind telling me why *I'm* here? If you say there has been no murder, then...well, I can't be here to solve it. There's no 'it' to solve.

PETER: Indeed. Well, now...very simply, John, you are here to make everybody else disappear. All my house guests. I want you to arrange it, somehow, so that they all leave, never return, and don't bother me again. Do you think you can do it?

JOHN: I'm sure I can. But wouldn't it have been easier not to invite them in the first place?

PETER: They'd have turned up anyway. They've been turning up for years. These people are obsessed with my mother.

Obsessed, I tell you! Swithun Kirk, the actor, wants me to sell him the film rights to Harriet's novel *The Heaviest Heart*, so that he can play its romantic hero. I've told him 'No' till I'm blue in the face. My mother was adamant that her novels should never be adapted for film or TV. She revered books and hated what was done to them in the supposedly good cause of screen adaptation.

JOHN: What about the other guests? Do they all want something?

PETER: (*indignantly*) Yes! They do! That blasted Irene Coggins is always under my feet, telling me how best to protect my mother's legacy, as if she knows more about it than I do. Professor Taylor constantly badgers me to find the missing letters for some research project she's engaged in. The art dealer lady, Tess Yolland, won't stop harassing me about Harriet's framed, unpublished books. She keeps offering me ever-larger sums of money if I'll sell them to her, so that she can sell them on at a profit to…I don't know…Charles Saatchi or Tracey Emin or someone like that. Max Russell would obviously love it if I gave permission for Harriet's four unpublished novels to be liberated from their frames and published after all these years.

JOHN: But your mother was determined that they should remain behind glass, never leave the house and never be read by anybody.

PETER: Yes, she was. And for a long time, I was equally determined that *I* should never leave the house. Whenever I did, there they all were, my tormentors – waiting outside to harangue me! Staying inside to avoid them didn't work either, though. They hammered at the door until Anders had no choice but to let them in. The noise they were making wasn't fair to the school in the garden. It disrupted lessons.

JOHN: So you want me to get rid of them all for you?

PETER: I do. Permanently. And I don't mean murder – not necessarily. (*He smiles*) I'm joking, of course. I just want them gone, and I'm willing to pay good money to make it happen. And then, once I'm rid of them, I don't want to see anyone or do anything for a jolly long while – especially not anything connected to being a famous writer's son!

SONG NO. 6: PETER'S LAMENT

PETER sings:

I dream that there will come a day, I'll open up my diary
And see no meeting, interview, appointment or enquiry,
No impossible decisions with ten minutes to decide in,
No queues of people keen to see the house my mother died in,
Just empty rooms and silence, peace and quiet for contemplation,
No frantic call from a festival that's planned a celebration
Of my mother's life and work or her enduring legacy
When I'd rather look round flats with Phil and Kirstie on TV.

I'm behind with all my viewing. Like, I've not seen Breaking Bad *yet.*
Not a single soul has noticed that I also had a dad yet,
Or that I'm a separate person who no longer wants to chat
About anti-genre snobbery or anything like that.
It's so tiring always smiling. I can feel the inner friction
Every time I claim to care that men don't read romantic fiction,
Every time I'm told to pose for photos by this library shelf.
How I yearn to board a ship and sail away all by myself.

I would rather not do anything, see anyone, go anywhere,
Not on any day, even one day out of ten.
I would rather not see even you, have a single easy thing to do,
I would rather not do anything, or see anyone again.
I would rather all my guests would leave. Tell 'em something that they'll all believe,
Say the house will soon run out of oxygen,
And a tear of joy will be in my eye when they pack their bags and say goodbye,
'Cause I'd rather not do anything, I'd rather not see anyone again.

JOHN sings:

You would rather not do anything, see anyone, go anywhere,
Not on any day, even one day out of ten.

PETER sings:

I would rather not see even you, have a single easy thing to do,

JOHN sings:

You would rather not do anything or see anyone again.
You would rather all your guests would leave…

PETER sings:

…Tell 'em something that they'll all believe,
Say the house will soon run out of oxygen,

BOTH sing:

And a tear of joy will be in my/your eye
When they pack their bags and say goodbye,
'Cause I'd/you'd rather not do anything, I'd/you'd rather not see anyone again.

JOHN: All right, I think I'm clear on the details. I'll shift your guests for you.

PETER: Thank you. And I'd appreciate it if you could do it tactfully. Make them think they lost interest of their own accord, if you know what I mean.

A scream comes from outside the room.

JOHN: What on earth was that?

PETER: (*rolling his eyes*) Who knows? Irene has probably noticed that Harriet's books aren't in the correct chronological order on a bookshelf somewhere. She is strongly of the view that alphabetical order is a terrible way to–

Enter CLEMENCY, wide-eyed and out of breath.

CLEM: He's dead, Peter!

PETER and JOHN freeze. They say nothing.

CLEM: (*clarifying*) I mean, not even a tiny bit alive any more. Quite thoroughly dead.

PETER: Who?

CLEM: The actor, Swithun Kirk. He's been murdered!

Lights go down.

SCENE 9

Police station. INSPECTOR COODE and SERGEANT WILDERSPIN are talking to a WOMAN who has come into the police station… Other WOMEN sneak in behind her. SERG W is taking notes in a notebook. The women look a bit strange – like the sort of women who might fall in love with famous killers in the hope that true love can cure psychopathy.

SERG W: (*to WOMAN*) And you say his name is…(*he looks at his notes*) Mr E?

WOMAN: That's what he calls himself online. I've come all the way from Fort Collins, Colorado to find him. He's a murderer and he's *famous*. He's got twenty-two thousand followers on Instagram. The other day he posted, 'Last few days of freedom, perhaps', and then, yesterday, 'Imminent arrest likely'.

INSP C: Have you considered the possibility that he's a fraud who's wasting everybody's time?

WOMAN: He never posts photos, obviously – only silhouettes – but you can tell he's gorgeous. (*Glances over her shoulder at the other women, who are listening eagerly.*) I don't care how many people he's killed as long as he doesn't cheat on me with other women who fall in love with famous murderers.

SERG W: I'm afraid I've never heard of him. He certainly isn't here, is he, boss?

INSP C: Most likely he's a figment of somebody's overactive imagination.

WOMAN: Oh, he's no figment. He's a legend…

SONG NO. 7: GREATEST FAN

WOMAN sings:

One day he'll arrive,
He'll be at your door,
And you'll ask him, what's his name?
Can your heart survive?
You won't know for sure
But you'll have to play his game,

And it's a lonely place
Without his face,
And it's an empty sound
When he's not around
And I'm the greatest fan
Of the mystery man.
Won't you say you love me,
Mr E?

Where the books are made
And the stories sold,
That was where he dreamed his plan.
If he'd never strayed
He'd grow wise and old
But he's not that kind of man.

And it's a lonely place
Without his face,
And it's an empty sound,
When he's not around
And I'm the greatest fan
Of the mystery man.
Won't you say you love me,
Mr E?

Oh, will you notice me tomorrow?
Oh, did you notice me today?
To win your love, I would beg, steal or borrow.
No one else has ever made me feel this way.

If I had the power
I would set you free.
I don't think you'd kill again.
Surely half an hour
Of true love from me
Could cure all murderous men,

All WOMEN sing:

And it's a lonely place
Mm-mm-mm
And it's an empty sound
Mm-mm-mm
And I'm your greatest fan
Mm-mm-mm
Won't you say you love me?

And it's a lonely place
Without his face
And it's an empty sound
When he's not around
And I'm the greatest fan
Of the mystery man.
Won't you say you love me
(Say you love me),
Mr E?

Lights go down.

END OF ACT ONE/INTERVAL

ACT TWO

SCENE 1

Police station. SERGEANT WILDERSPIN is doing paperwork. INSPECTOR COODE is on the phone.

INSP C: (*on phone*) Idlewyld House? Yes, I know where it is. A murder, you say?…A general *what*? (*He sighs*) I see. (*Disapprovingly*) No, nothing surprises me any more. And your name is? Clemency… I beg your pardon? No, I'm afraid I haven't heard of you… Well, I wouldn't know anything about that. Hello? (*He looks at the phone. Clearly CLEMENCY LANDRIGAN has hung up on him. He hangs up the phone.*)

INSP C: (*to SERG W*) That was a Mrs Landrigan. There's been a murder at Idlewyld House. There's apparently a man called John Danes already at the house who believes he can solve the crime without our help. Do you want to hear the best part, Sergeant?

SERG W: Yes please, boss.

INSP C: He is no sort of detective – not even an amateur one. He calls himself 'The Generalist'. From the description given to me by Clemency Landrigan, he sounds like a tiresome impostor. Ah well – we'll soon put him in his place.

SERG W: (*impressed*) Not Clemency Landrigan the perfume designer?

INSP C: You've heard of her, then? As I was about to tell her when she rudely hung up on me, the names of perfume designers are of no use to me.

SERG W: Right, boss – because you're a bloke!

INSP C: (*sighs*). I *am* a bloke – well observed, sergeant – but that's not what I meant. I was referring to a rare condition I suffer from. Had it since birth. It's called Anosmia.

SONG NO. 8: CLUE-MONT

INSP C sings:

I've been anosmic all my life,
Young sidekick Sergeant Wilderspin.
No gels, no pills, no surgeon's knife
And no pink-pepper flavoured gin
Can help me. It's my nose I blame –
It's such a sad, sad tale to tell:
The food I eat all tastes the same.
I lack a working sense of smell.
I have no sense of smell…

Wait, though, before you feel downcast
On my unfortunate behalf.
Let me succinctly tell you why
I'm often more inclined to laugh.
You've heard, I trust, that when one sense
Declines or fails, the others thrive?
I have become, ladies and gents,
The very finest sleuth alive.
I'm now the greatest sleuth alive.

I arrive at each denouement,
And I walk into the room-ont
And immediately know who-mont
Is the one that did the deed.

While he yells 'To hell with you-mont!'
I explain what's false and true-mont
From my expert point of view-mont
And success is guaranteed,
Yes, success is guaranteed.

SERG W: That's all very well, boss, but what if the culprit isn't in the room? What if he's elsewhere?

INSP C sings:

Dear oh dear, what can one do-mont
With a sidekick thick and new-mont,
If his judgement's all askew-mont,
Like young Sergeant Wilderspin?

(Points to audience)

They all know, and so should you-mont:
If the scene is the denouement,
In a plane, train, boat or room-ont,
That's a scene the culprit's in,
It's a scene the culprit's in.

He or she might be a rotter,
Evil genius, murder plotter…
Come denouement time, he's gotta
Find himself a comfy chair
In the circle. His accuser
Then reveals why he's the loser –
Monstrous fiend or hapless bruiser
He will never be elsewhere.
He must never be elsewhere.

SERG W: Boss, shouldn't we be on our way? Before John Danes the Generalist ruins everything with his lack of official credentials?

INSP C sings:

Slow down, sergeant, what's the hurry?
I don't think we need to worry,
For the spicy smell of curry
Or a brand new bright red rose
Will distract this John Danes feller,
He'll be weak if he's a smeller.
We anosmics have to tell a
Chap what's right beneath his nose,
When it's right beneath his nose.

Mister Danes will cry boohoo-mont,
We'll show him a thing or two-mont,
He'll be grateful he withdrew-mont.
Let the Generalist begin
To discover that in lieu-mont
Of the well-trained boys in blue-mont
He's as useless as a clue-mont
With no puzzle to be in,
With no puzzle to be in...

JOHN DANES enters while the above chorus is being sung. He is clearly not at the police station, but outside of that scene. He walks to the front of the stage and addresses the audience, singing:

They're on their way: Inspector Coode
And Sergeant Wilderspin.
One's quite naive. The other dude
Seems to think he's starring in

A story that plays by the rules,
And respects authority.
I can't wait for these two fools to meet
Oscar Landrigan and me.

JOHN, INSP C, SERG W and POLICE CHORUS sing:

Da-da-da-da-da denouement,
Da-da-da-da-da-da room-ont,
Da-da-da-da-da-da who-mont,
Da-da-da-da-did-the-deed,
Da-da-da-da-hell-with-you-mont,
Da-da-da-da false-and-true-mont,
Da-da-da-da point-of-view-mont,
Da-da-da-da guaranteed,

JOHN exits.

INSP C sings, pensively and slowly:

There are things one can assume-ont:
Ideal bride or perfect groom-ont,

(he picks up the pace as between five and ten other uniformed police officers enter and gather round to listen)

Wedding vows like magic glue-mont
In a romance worth its salt.
We policemen have one forte:
It's to catch those who've been nor-tay.
With the full force of the law-tay,
We make clear it's all their fault.
(It is always all their fault.)

INSP C, SERG W and POLICE CHORUS sing:

Da-da-da-da-da boo-hoo-mont,
Da-da-da-da thing or two-mont,
Da-da-da-da-da withdrew-mont,
Da-da-da-da-da begin,
Da-da-da-da-da in-lieu-mont,
Da-da-da-da boys-in-blue-mont,
Da-da-da-da-da-da clue-mont
With no puzzle to be in,
With no puzzle to be in.

INSP C sings:

I've been anosmic all my life,
Young sidekick Sergeant Wilderspin…

SERG W: You have, sir. Since the day you were born.

INSP C: (*puzzled*) There's no need to tell me what I've just told you, sergeant. Now, I'm going to Idlewyld House to solve a murder. You may accompany me if you wish. If you do, please try to be useful and don't just repeat everything I say.

SERG W: Don't just repeat…oh. Right. Got it, boss.

INSP C exits. SERG W grabs notebook and pen and hurries after him.

SCENE 2

Drawing room at Idlewyld House. Present are: PETER LANDRIGAN, OSCAR LANDRIGAN, JOHN DANES, PROF LAURA TAYLOR, IRENE COGGINS, MAX RUSSELL, TESS YOLLAND.

Enter CLEMENCY LANDRIGAN, followed by ANDERS, who is carrying his bunch of keys.

CLEM: The police are on their way. And…I'm afraid there's more bad news.

JOHN: Not another murder?

CLEM: No. It's your hat and coat, John. They're ruined. Swithun Kirk was wearing them when he was stabbed. Both are covered in blood.

JOHN: Why would he put on my hat and coat?

CLEM: He's an actor. *Was* an actor, I should say. (*Tearfully*) He loved nothing more than to try on clothes that weren't his.

IRENE: Yes, he was forever snatching my scarf and draping it round his neck!

JOHN: Where was he stabbed?

CLEM: In the hall. At the bottom of the stairs.

JOHN: No, I mean where on *him* – his chest, his stomach?

ANDERS: He was stabbed in the back with great force. (*With obvious gory relish*) The knife's blade went right through his heart.

Everyone looks suspiciously at ANDERS. He does his best to look innocent.

JOHN: (*stands*) So the killer didn't see Kirk's face. He stabbed him from behind. That means… I believe that means it was *me* he meant to kill! He saw my hat and coat and assumed I was the person inside them.

ANDERS: How would he have known they were yours? No one saw you wearing them apart from me…

Everyone once again regards ANDERS with suspicion.

ANDERS: …and I didn't murder anybody.

JOHN: You're wrong, Anders. Someone else *did* see me wearing them – Mr E.

IRENE: Who?

JOHN: Before I set off to come here, a stranger called at my house, a man who called himself 'Mr E'. He told me he was the murderer, without mentioning any details of his alleged crime or crimes. I thought there were three possibilities: he was either mad, or he was joking, or he was talking about a murder he'd already committed. But what if he was referring to a murder he intended to commit in the future?

OSCAR: The Mystery of Mr E!

CLEM: Be quiet, Oscar, darling. You're a child – you shouldn't be listening to conversations about brutal murders. (*Frowns, then realises she's solved the problem*) Be a good boy and pretend you're not listening!

PETER: John and I were in the library together when Kirk was stabbed, so we're in the clear. Where was everybody else?

ANDERS: I was in the kitchen with Oscar, making him a sandwich. Ham and pickle.

OSCAR: Were you?

ANDERS: Yes. Remember, I handed it to you? You said, 'TY' and I said 'NP'?

JOHN: TY and NP?

ANDERS: 'Thank you' and 'No problem'. Oscar prefers to avoid using whole words if at all possible.

OSCAR: Whole words? (*He snorts derisively, not impressed, and shakes his head*) Long, bruv.

ANDERS: (*furious, clipped*) Not all words are long, Oscar. I can think of two that are very short indeed, the first of which begins with an F–

OSCAR: (*as enlightenment dawns*) Wait! That's right! We *were* in the kitchen together. First you asked me if I couldn't get myself a snack for once instead of making you do it, and I said 'CBA'.

CLEM: CBA? What does that mean, darling?

ANDERS: (*to audience*) Complete Brain Atrophy.

OSCAR: It means 'Can't be arsed', mum.

CLEM: (*laughing, presses her hands against her heart*) Oh, how adorable! (*Serious again*) Well, all right, so we know where Peter, John, Oscar and Anders were at the time of the murder. And the rest of us – Professor Taylor, Tess, Max, Irene, and me – we were all in here. (*To MAX*) I was telling you about Oscar's school.

MAX: You were. None of us left the room.

JOHN: So it seems nobody could have killed Swithun Kirk. Everyone is accounted for. Apart from Mr E.

ANDERS: How would your Mr E have got in? The windows and doors were all closed and locked.

JOHN: Are you sure?

ANDERS: Absolutely. (*Waves bunch of keys in the air.*) I check all the locks twice an hour.

CLEM: I insist upon it, as a preventative measure – so that Oscar's French teacher, Mrs Lapp, can't sneak in and plant incriminating evidence among his possessions. She's tried before.

PROF. T: Then…it seems no one can have done it. Unless…

TESS: Are you thinking what I'm thinking, Professor? A conspiracy?

PROF. T: (*sheepishly*) Well, yes. Peter and John could have done it together. Or perhaps Oscar and Anders conspired to commit murder. We know that *our* group didn't, of course…but those who weren't part of our group don't know that.

JOHN: You're all discounting Mr E too easily. The man came to my house and *told* me he was the murderer.

MAX: It won't be him, then. That's too obvious.

JOHN: It's not obvious at all. We have no idea who he is!

IRENE: Good point.

MAX: What about motive? I can't see that any of us would have one. Swithun was annoying...pompous...utterly self-absorbed. I mean, you could be bleeding from the eyeballs and he'd barely notice...but none of that's a good enough reason to kill a man.

JOHN: Who found the body?

CLEM: I did.

TESS: Wait – I know what you're thinking, Mr Danes. Perhaps Clemency left the room, stabbed Swithun and then (*makes air quotes*) *found* his body? Impossible! She opened the door and immediately screamed, while she was still in here with us. We all rushed over and saw the very same horrible sight: Swithun Kirk lying dead on the floor in a large pool of blood.

CLEM: Oscar, dear, run along to the library and have a go at doing your French homework.

OSCAR: I hid it in a book, like you told me to. I've forgotten which one.

CLEM: Oh. Well, do other homework, then. Haven't you got Scripture, and Chemistry?

OSCAR: Yeah. And History and Geography. But I want to help solve the mystery of Mr E.

CLEM: No! Sorry, darling, but murder isn't something an innocent young boy should be thinking about.

OSCAR: But I think I can help! There's this book in the library called–

CLEM: (*talking over him*) If you don't want to do homework, go and have a snappy chat with your friends or whatever you call it.

OSCAR: (*head in hands*) OMG, why are parents so annoying?

(*Walks to front of stage, pulling his iPhone out of his pocket, and starts texting…*)

PETER LANDRIGAN, JOHN DANES, PROF LAURA TAYLOR, IRENE COGGINS, MAX RUSSELL, TESS YOLLAND, CLEMENCY LANDRIGAN and ANDERS all exit.

Enter ASBO, 3-STRIKE and FONDER, all carrying iPhones. ASBO stands next to OSCAR at the front of the stage. The others stand behind them.

OSCAR: (*talking slowly, as he types each word*) Hey…ASBO… what…you…doing? Have…you…hidden…all…your… homework…yet? Send.

ASBO: (talking slowly, while texting…) Yo, blood. Not…
gonna…be…hiding…homework…no…more.
Someone…might…find it and…try to…make me do it.
Am gonna be…burning all my homework…from now
on, and feeding the ashes…to the cat. And if anyone…
tries to stop me…they's gonna get shanked. Send.

OSCAR: That just happened…at my house. Send.

ASBO: You crack me…up, blood. Laughing emoji. Send.

OSCAR: For real…Guest at ours just got shanked…and guess what my mum said? 'Go and do your homework, Oscar'. Send.

3-STRIKE: Rude word parents. Send.

OSCAR: Quite exceptionally rude word parents…Even ruder word homework. Send.

FONDER: (*slowly*) String of currently fashionable, misspelt obscenities without any punctuation. Send.

(*OSCAR and all others put their phones away in their pockets.*)

SONG NO. 9: I'D MUCH PREFER TO SOLVE A MYSTERY

OSCAR sings:

Do they think it's realistic
To say 'Do your homework, child'?
I would answer them, but no one really cares.
Chances are there's a sadistic
Killer here at Idlewyld
Dropping corpses at the bottom of our stairs –

OSCAR and ASBO sing:

A significant distraction
From the chemical reaction

That occurs when hydro-what's-it-called meets lead.
I've got Scripture prep for Monday
But I'll have a more well-done day
If I help to catch a murderer instead.

OSCAR, ASBO and the others sing:

Let the conscientious learners
Form strong bonds with Bunsen Burners
And debate Guy Fawkes and other cutlery.
If you want to sketch a toucan
From some dull rain-forest, you can,
But I'd much prefer to solve a mystery!

OSCAR sings:

If I never reach Kings College
Where they stuff you full of knowledge,
If I never make St John's or Trinity,

ASBO sings:

I'll just head right back to Pffisham
And explain that it's John Grisham,
Not John Dalton, who I'd really like to be.

OSCAR sings:

The dead man's an Oscar winner,
And since Oscar is my name,
It's quite natural that it should fall to me
To detect a lurking sinner
And apportion heaps of blame
To the cryptic and nefarious Mr E!

OSCAR and ASBO sing:

A significant distraction
From the chemical reaction
That occurs when hydro-blah-di-blah meets lead.
I've got Scripture prep for Monday
But I'll have a more well-done day
If I help to catch a murderer instead.

OSCAR, ASBO, 3-STRIKE and FONDER sing:

Let the conscientious learners
Form strong bonds with Bunsen Burners
And debate Guy Fawkes and other cutlery.
If you want to sketch a toucan
From some dull rain-forest, you can,
But I'd much prefer to solve a mystery!
But I'd much prefer…to solve…a mystery!

OSCAR, ASBO, 3-STRIKE and FONDER exit, and we're back to the Drawing Room at Idlewyld House. Enter PETER LANDRIGAN, CLEMENCY LANDRIGAN, ANDERS, JOHN DANES, PROFESSOR LAURA TAYLOR, IRENE COGGINS, MAX RUSSELL, TESS YOLLAND.

JOHN: What about the murder weapon? Was it there, at the scene of the crime?

CLEM: No. There was no sign of a knife or anything sharp.

JOHN: Tell me, what made you go and open the door to the hall? And why wasn't Swithun Kirk in here with the rest of you? What made him leave the room?

CLEM: (*Pause as she thinks hard.*) Gosh, yes, how clever of you! Swithun had gone to the kitchen in search of booze, but he'd closed the drawing room door behind him. I opened it because…well, I didn't think of it until now, but I heard the front door lock. Or unlock. Definitely the front door, though. We weren't expecting anyone else, so I wondered who it was. Goodness me! That's significant, isn't it?

JOHN: It might be, yes. You might have heard the murderer leaving. Let's say he took the knife with him, closed and locked the door and made himself scarce… He'd have needed a key.

Everyone looks at the keys ANDERS is carrying. ANDERS notices, and hides them behind his back.

PETER: Hold on a minute, John. Let's say you're right and this mysterious Mr E killed Swithun Kirk, believing him to be you. What was his motive? Why did he want you dead?

MAX: That's a good question.

JOHN: It is – and I don't know the answer. *Yet.* But I will, and hopefully before the police get here. It would be nice to present them with a solved case, all neat and tidy.

PROF. T: Perhaps when this Mr E told you that he was the murderer, he meant to suggest that he was *your* murderer – that he intended to kill *you.*

JOHN: I don't think so. He said he wanted to catch me – to present me with an impossible-to-solve puzzle, so that I'd become obsessed. There's no time for that to happen if he kills me the very same day.

IRENE: But then whose murderer did he intend to imply that he was? Until Swithun Kirk, there was no victim.

PROF. T: (*insistently*) Perhaps there was.

JOHN: (*thoughtfully*) Anders, can you unlock the front door and let me out? I'd like to take a stroll around the gardens. It'll help me to think clearly. The rest of you, stay here, together. Keep talking – see if you can come up with anything useful.

Exit JOHN.

SCENE 3

The gardens of Idlewyld House.

Enter JOHN

Enter PROF TAYLOR, running after him.

PROF. T: Mr Danes! Wait!

JOHN: (*turns*) Do call me John. What should I call you?

PROF. T: I'm Professor Laura Taylor, so how about…Professor Taylor? (*Relenting somewhat*) You could call me Prof, I suppose.

JOHN: Prof. I like it (*smiles*). Why'd you come running after me?

PROF. T: I've got a theory. I think Harriet Landrigan was murdered. I don't believe she fell down the stairs by accident.

JOHN: You could be right – but what makes you so sure?

PROF. T: (*defensive*) Well, she obviously had a secret – one she wrote about in those letters to her publisher that were stolen from the archive.

JOHN: Go on.

PROF T: (*a little sheepish*). I mean…people who have secrets often get murdered, don't they?

JOHN: (*sceptically*) That's probably truer in reverse: people who get murdered often have – or had – secrets. I see your point, but it's hardly proof, is it?

PROF. T: And then there's your Mr E. I think it was *Harriet* that he murdered! *And* Swithun Kirk.

JOHN: Again…where's the proof?

PROF. T: (*desperately, pushing him as she speaks*) *You* need to *find* the proof!

JOHN: Why do you care so much?

OSCAR wanders on to the stage behind them, looking at his iPhone.

PROF. T: That's none of your business. (*Long pause, during which JOHN nudges her, gives her a winning smile and raises an eyebrow at her. She relents.*) It's my current research project. I'm writing a monograph in which I argue that crime novelists are more likely to fall in love, while romantic novelists are more likely to get murdered.

JOHN: I see. So you're a Literature Professor?

PROF. T: English Literature, Cultural History and Psychology. I'm interdisciplinary.

JOHN: (*grinning*) You're a Generalist, like me!

PROF. T: I'm in trouble, is what I am. I need Harriet Landrigan to have been murdered or else my theory doesn't hold water.

JOHN: Aren't you approaching it the wrong way round? I mean…shouldn't you look at the evidence, or the data or whatever, and *then* formulate a theory?

PROF. T: (*shoots him a scathing look*) You wouldn't last five minutes in academia.

JOHN: Why don't you wait till I find out the truth about this whole strange business? Then write a monograph about that – whatever I find out. I bet you could get a brilliant book out of it. You could interview me extensively. In years to come, people will say, 'Professor Laura Taylor wrote the definitive book about the mysterious case of Harriet Landrigan, Swithun Kirk and Mr E.'

PROF. T: (*suddenly unhappy*) No one will ever say I did anything definitive, or even halfway decent. And frankly, I'm sick of trying. I don't know if I can do it any more.

JOHN: Course you can! You just need to believe in yourself. Be optimistic.

PROF. T: Optimistic? (*Sarcastically*) Hah – you're funny. What's the point in kidding myself? I might as well face facts…

SONG NO. 10: SOMETHING WRONG

PROF. T sings:

One more false start,
One torn-up chart,
There's no place left to go.
One more dead end –
I can't pretend
That next time I'll just know
How to advance,
Adapt my plans,
Or how to solve it when
There's something wrong,
There's something wrong,
There's something wrong again.

It's like a rail –
Along I sail
Until I hit the wall.
It's like a dream –
How real they seem –
I fly, then freeze and fall.
Dreams don't come good.
I wish they would,
But nine times out of ten,
There's something wrong,
There's something wrong,
There's something wrong again.

JOHN sings, sarcastically:

I must admit
Your plan to quit
Is one that I applaud.
Your urgent need
To unsucceed
Is not remotely flawed.
Your every move
Just goes to prove
You lack true acumen

JOHN puts on a girly whiny voice and sings:

There's something wrong,
There's something wrong,
There's something wrong again.

JOHN moves away from PROF. T and sings to audience:

Why do I try
To make her cry,
To make her start anew?
Why do I feel,
As if they're real,
The great things she could do?
Why do I care?
It hurts right here.
I might need Nurofen.
There's something wrong,
There's something wrong,
There's something wrong again.

PROF. T sings, sarcastic and angry:

It's such a treat,
So nice to meet
The man who knows it all!
That cut above,
Don't fall in love –
You've miles and miles to fall.
My heart has missed
A 'Generalist'
Who'll tell me what to do.
There's something wrong,
There's something wrong,
There's something wrong…with you!

PROF. T sings to audience:

Why is my rage
So fake, so staged?
My heart chimes like Big Ben.

There's something wrong,
There's something wrong,
There's something wrong with men.
All this I know
But even so
He's right here with me when
There's nothing wrong...
There's nothing wrong,
There's nothing wrong again,

JOHN walks towards her. He sings:

There's nothing wrong.
There's nothing wrong,

BOTH, moving closer to one another, sing:

There's nothing... wrong... again.

OSCAR: (*walking over to them, interrupting their almost-romantic moment*) Yo, Prof.

PROF. T: Yes, Oscar?

OSCAR: Why don't you hide this... thing you're supposed to be writing, like I always hide my homework? Then no one'll expect you to finish it. You can say you haven't got a clue where it is. It doesn't matter that you're not a child. Grown-ups hide things in our library too.

JOHN: (*with keen interest*) What do you mean, Oscar?

OSCAR: Once when I tried to hide my Maths homework in a book, I found a load of letters had been stuffed in there already.

JOHN: (*to OSCAR*) Letters?

OSCAR: Yeah. They're hidden in a book called *The Mystery of Mr E*. That's what I was trying to say, before Mum told me not to talk about murder. I thought the letters might have something to do with Swithun Kirk's death, because… well, because of your mysterious visitor, Mr E, who said he was a murderer, and the title of the book. When I put the two together…

JOHN: (*excited*) It certainly sounds as if these letters might be very relevant indeed. Oscar, you're a star!

OSCAR: No, I'm not. Bartie Voss at my school – *he's* a star. Mum likes to think I am too, and I let her believe it, but the truth is, I'm a hopeless ne'er-do-well and that's all I'll ever be. Ask Anders – he'll tell you. He tells *me* all the time.

PROF. T: (*angry on OSCAR's behalf.*) That's disgraceful. What sort of person says that to a child?

JOHN: Anders is wrong, Oscar.

PROF. T: Next time he tells you that, smile innocently and say, 'Anders, when you were my age, did you dream of locking and unlocking someone else's front door for a living?'

OSCAR: (*laughing*) Sick burn!

PROF. T: What's wrong? (C*oncerned, looking around*) Are you sick? Did someone burn you?

JOHN: No one burned him, Prof. He means… you know. Shade thrown. Shots fired.

PROF. T: Gunshots? Where? Quick, everybody duck!

OSCAR: (*to JOHN*) Is she from, like, 1995 or something?

JOHN: Oscar, you're a very clever and rather amusing boy. I think you'll go far.

OSCAR: I'm not sure I want to go *far*. That sounds tiring. But I can take you to the library and show you the hidden letters if you like?

JOHN: Great. Laura, you go back to the drawing room and keep everybody in there. Oscar and I don't want to be disturbed.

PROF. T: Did I say you could call me Laura?

JOHN: (*grinning*) No, but I seem to have managed to do it anyway.

PROF. T: How can I keep everyone in the drawing room? What if one of them wants to leave?

JOHN: Stop them.

PROF. T: (*thoughtfully*) I might invite them to speculate about *why*. The framed books, I mean. That's what fascinates me, far more than any murders. Why would the most popular romantic novelist in the world decide to carry on writing but never publish a book again? What can have happened to her to make her behave so oddly? Did she want to write about a guilty secret, maybe, that she'd kept for years? Or perhaps she was simply fed up of writing and didn't want to do it anymore. She couldn't bring herself to admit it, so she pretended to carry on, but in fact all the framed books are totally empty – blank pages!

JOHN: Fascinating! I hadn't thought of that last possibility. You have a powerful imagination – and I mean that as a compliment.

PROF. T: (*embarrassed*) Thank you. Though one might argue that praise from a stranger means very little.

JOHN: Or one might just say 'Thank you' and then shut up? Now, go back to the house and keep them all speculating about the framed books until the police arrive. Come on, Oscar – to the library!

JOHN and OSCAR exit. Once they've gone, PROF. T exits more slowly.

SCENE 4

Idlewyld House Library. There's a table with a pile of books on it. Enter OSCAR and JOHN. OSCAR picks up a book from the pile on the table and hands it to JOHN. It's called The Mystery of Mr E.

JOHN: Well, well: *The Mystery of Mr E*...(*suddenly startled*) Holy Pfffff...isham School!

OSCAR: What?

JOHN: This book is by DeVaux Russell. Deevo – Harriet's publisher. That's right: your father said Deevo wrote thrillers. Rather violent ones, he said. This must be one of them.

OSCAR: Good old Deevo.

JOHN: Why do you say that?

OSCAR: If it weren't for him, I'd have nowhere to hide my homework. Deevo had this library specially built for my grandmother, to celebrate her selling ten million books. I mean...ten million *copies*. She obviously didn't write ten million books. I wasn't born yet, but Dad told me about it. It was a surprise present. Top secret. They all went away on holiday – Grandmother, Dad, Mum and Anders – and when they got back, this library was here. Full of books, too.

JOHN: (*Not paying attention, flicking through the pages of* The Mystery of Mr E) Oscar, have you read this book?

OSCAR: Nah. CBA.

JOHN: (*He pulls out a bundle of letters from the book.*) You must have read these when you found them, though, right?

OSCAR: Nope.

JOHN: Really? That's good. It's safer not to. There's a good chance that the secret contained in these letters has caused at least one murder. (*He starts to read the letters.*)

OSCAR: That actually makes me want to read them. Weird. I've never wanted to read anything before. Can I read them after you?

JOHN: (*Staring incredulously at the letters as he reads*) Oh, my goodness. Wow.

OSCAR: Give them to me! Give! Me!

JOHN: Oscar, I need you to do something important for me. Do you think you could turn your hand to a spot of vandalism?

OSCAR: Like what?

JOHN: Your grandmother's framed books – the unpublished ones. I need you to smash the glass and get them out.

OSCAR: I can't. I'd get grounded, like, for ever.

JOHN: Would you? I reckon your mum'd let you get away with anything.

OSCAR: *She* would. Dad wouldn't.

JOHN: I see. Yes, of course. It was unfair of me to ask. It's just... I need to have a look at those books. (*Slowly*) I *think* I've just worked out who killed whom and why, but for the sake of completeness, I need to see what's in those four unpublished novels that Harriet didn't want anyone to read.

OSCAR: My mate ASBO'd be happy to smash things up for you, but he'd leave devastation in his wake. (*Brightens up)* I know who could get into the books without anyone knowing: Bartie Voss! Pffisham School's star pupil. I'll go over to school now and get him.

JOHN: But then Bartie will get in trouble.

OSCAR: No, he won't. He'll know how to get the books out so that you can have a look at them, and then repair the glass so that no one'll know it was ever smashed. He can also speed-read the books for you if you like. And he'll be able to do it all in about ten minutes.

JOHN: (*looks at his watch*) Will he still be at school, at this time?

OSCAR: Definitely. We get our reports tomorrow, which means the teachers will be writing them tonight. Bartie'll be helping them. They're not supposed to, but everyone knows they let him hang around in the staffroom and laugh at the reports that are worse than his – which is all of them. Not only mine.

JOHN: If Bartie really is Pffisham School's star pupil, surely he won't want to smash up someone else's possessions?

OSCAR: You don't know Bartie. He'll do anything as long as he can be seen to do it brilliantly. He doesn't care about being good, only about being the best. I've always said to him: if he'd just concentrate on being great at things he's not supposed to be doing at all, he could join my gang. Come on, you persuade Anders to let me out and I'll head over to school.

SCENE 5

Pffisham School Staffroom. Papers on tables, including some colourful bar charts. BARTIE is in the staffroom, with his feet up, being fussed over by adoring teachers MISS NEARY and MR MORRISON. He is laughing at less able pupils' reports. OSCAR approaches. He looks through the open window, from outside…

BARTIE: I like the way you say Tobias Boland 'could do better', Miss. It's kinder than saying 'He could hardly do worse', I suppose.

(*BARTIE, MISS NEARY and MR MORRISON all laugh*)

MR M: Who's next?

BARTIE: (*consults list*) William Chadwick.

MISS N: Ugh. His parents will insist on changing every word, no matter what we write.

MR M: I thought we'd phased out words and were just doing these weird coloured bands now (*He holds up an example of a bar chart.*) Much easier! Speaking of which…have we decided yet what we're going to pretend this year's weird coloured bands mean?

BARTIE: We have, sir. A green bar means 'Nearly, but not quite, as good as Bartie Voss'. *(They all laugh.)* Blue means 'Meh'. Yellow means 'I'm so done', and this year we've introduced a new lowest category: mauve, which means 'I can't even'.

MR M: And we're not worried that some parents might find those definitions a little…unclear?

MISS N: What does it matter, really? Mr Friend always lets the most difficult parents rewrite their children's reports to make them more favourable. We might as well make them all multiple choice!

SONG NO. 11: PLEASE FIND ENCLOSED

MISS N picks up a nearby report and sings:

Dear parents, carers, guardians of
(Insert the child's name here),
Your child (insert child's name again)
Has had a term-filled year
He's thick and toxic (forward-slash)
A credit to Year 8,
And has a diverse group of friends
(Slash) not one single mate
(Slash) We're not quite sure who he is
(Delete as appropriate).
(Weird coloured band) Please send twelve grand
By (insert a scary date).

MR M sits down and starts to write a report, singing:

Please find enclosed the school report
Of Oscar from Year 9 –

(OSCAR looks alarmed. Starts to fish in his pockets for a piece of paper and a pen.)

MR M sings:

Heir to a great big fortune, so
He'll basically be fine.
That's lucky, as this document
You now hold in your hands
Consists of random coloured bars
That no-one understands.
One bar of blue. Green – not for you!
For our stellar student brands.
We have no choice. Here's our invoice.
Don't make any more demands.

(OSCAR is writing…)

MISS N and MR M sing:

We're educated people, all –
Minds full of useful thoughts
Which we make sure not to include
In any school reports.
Instead, we send you something that
Mark Rothko might have done,
Drunk while on Microsoft Excel
To sabotage for fun
Each mother's need to sit and read
Cogent facts about her son.
One bar of mauve? Blame Michael Gove
Like you know we've always done.
We have no choice. Here's our invoice.
Yes, that's right, another one.

OSCAR: (*shouts through window*) Bartie! I need your help. It's important, and no one but you can do it!

BARTIE: (*with supreme confidence*) Of *course* they can't. How may I be of assistance?

OSCAR: Actually, there's two things… (*hands him the piece of paper he's been writing on*). First, you need to substitute this for my real report – the one Mr Morrison's just written.

BARTIE: Why?

OSCAR: Because my version's more…upbeat. When they go low, I go high.

BARTIE: (*frowns*) Well, I wouldn't normally…

OSCAR: (*charmingly*) But if you did, you would surely bring an unparalleled degree of flair and aplomb to the task – am I right?

BARTIE: I suppose, just this once… (*He takes OSCAR's version of the report, puts it with the others, and throws away OSCAR's original report. MR MORRISON and MISS NEARY don't notice.*)

OSCAR: Cheers, mate. And now you're going to help us catch a murderer. Come on!

(*BARTIE climbs out of the window and exits with OSCAR, as MISS NEARY finds OSCAR's fake report – the one he's written himself – and starts to sing…*)

MISS N sings:

Please find enclosed the school report
Of Oscar Landrigan.
He's a delightful boy. One day
He'll be a lovely man.
We understand well why he yawns
And doesn't do a thing.
We know those lessons which he scorns
Should be more interesting.
Every schoolmarm falls for his charm.
He's a sweetheart, he's a dear.
How hard we'd grieve, were he to leave.
We would pay to keep him here.
These are our thoughts. No more reports.
Read this one again next year.

SCENE 6

Drawing Room at Idlewyld House. Enter JOHN and OSCAR. Everyone else (PETER, CLEMENCY, ANDERS, MAX, IRENE, TESS and PROF TAYLOR) is already there, including two newcomers: INSPECTOR COODE and SERGEANT WILDERSPIN. INSPECTOR COODE projects a strong air of disdain throughout. SERGEANT WILDERSPIN has a notebook and pen and is jotting everything down.

INSP C: So. You must be John Danes, the Generalist.

JOHN: In general, I would say that's true.

INSP C: I'm Inspector Coode. This is Sergeant Wilderspin.

JOHN: Good to meet you both. I'm sorry you've had a wasted trip.

INSP C: Wasted trip? I was told there had been a murder.

SERG W: (*to INSP C*) The Generalist says we've had a wasted trip, boss.

JOHN: There has indeed been a murder – but I've just solved it, so there's really no need for you to be here.

INSP C: So the murderer has been detained, then?

JOHN: Oh... No! Sorry. I forgot about the boring administrative things that need to happen once the mystery's solved. Perhaps you two could take care of that part? I don't have the authority to arrest anyone.

SERG W: (*to INSP C*) He wants us to arrest the killer, boss.

INSP C: (*to JOHN*) You've solved the mystery, you say? I've never heard of a Generalist solving a murder.

JOHN: Actually, I've solved two murders. And I bet you'd never heard of a Generalist at all until you heard about me. Well, had you?

INSP C: (*disapprovingly*) No. I had not. 'And I'll admit, that was a state of affairs I enjoyed greatly.

SERG W: (*to INSP C*) He reckons he's solved *two* murders, boss.

JOHN: I have. Swithun Kirk wasn't the first victim. That was Harriet Landrigan, in 2004. She didn't fall down the stairs. She was pushed to her death by a determined killer.

IRENE: (*leaps to her feet*) Who? Tell me who and I'll rip his heart out with my bare hands.

PETER: Come now, Irene... Getting hysterical isn't going to–

IRENE: Shut up! You have no idea of the *agonies* I suffer! I am a lifelong, devoted *fan*! *You're* only her son!

PETER: (*half hurt, half puzzled by the irrationality*) I'm not sure that's entirely fair...

INSP C: Everybody be quiet. No emoting, please, until I've been apprised of all the facts. Tell me everything, Mr Danes. First of all, who is the murderer?

JOHN: I don't know his name, but I will very soon. And I can tell you now that Harriet Landrigan and Swithun Kirk were both killed by the same person – the man who announced himself to me as 'the murderer'. Let's call him Mr E, although arguably he lied about that.

INSP C: What do you mean, 'arguably'?

JOHN: Normally we'd assume that someone calling himself Mr E would have E as the first letter of his *last* name. That is not true of our Mr E. His last name begins with a different letter of the alphabet. E is the first letter of his *first* name.

CLEM: But surely, if you know all that then you must know who he is?

JOHN: Sort of, yes. But not quite.

SERG W: The Generalist sort of knows who the killer is, boss. But not quite.

INSP C: I heard him, Sergeant. As I suspected, his methods appear to be laughably haphazard. I didn't get where I am today by *sort of* knowing who the murderer is. Mr Danes, do you know what we in the major crimes unit called 'sort of solved' crimes? Do you want to tell him, Sergeant?

SERG W: (*Looks up…*) Hm? Oh, yes, boss. We call them 'unsolved.'

INSP C: (*very sneery and sarcastic*) That is correct. We call them… unsolved.

JOHN: Give me a minute, Inspector. I'm getting there. Let me introduce you to Max Russell. He might be able to help us.

MAX: Me? How can I help?

JOHN: Anders and Peter have both told me that one of the people now running your publishing firm is your cousin: Deevo Russell's nephew. Does his first name begin with an E?

MAX: (*puzzled*) No. His name is Frederick. Freddie, we call him.

JOHN: (*pondering*) Hmmm. That, I'm afraid, rules him out.

INSP C: So…it's *not* Frederick Russell, then?

JOHN: Definitely not.

SERG W: (*writing in a notebook*) 'Not…Frederick…Russell.' The Generalist doesn't seem to think it's Frederick Russell, boss.

INSP C: I heard him, Sergeant. I am, in fact, in the room, and I have ears. Just as you are; just as you do. (*To JOHN*) Tell us who the killer is, then, Mr Danes, so that I know whom to arrest.

JOHN: Cripes. I don't know where to start. All right, let's go back to the beginning. I was getting ready to come here when a man appeared and identified himself to me as 'the murderer'. He mentioned Idlewyld House. He knew I was coming here. I thought I might find a murder here, waiting for me to solve it – a murder he had committed

– but when I arrived, I was told that nothing of the sort had occurred. I was perplexed by this, of course…until I heard from Peter Landrigan that his mother – the late, great Harriet – had died *by accident* after having behaved most peculiarly for a number of years in relation to her novels: refusing to publish them, refusing to explain why. Naturally, I wondered if her supposedly accidental death might be the murder I was meant to solve. I *then* discovered that her publisher, Deevo Russell, had died one year before she did. One year '*almost to the day*' – those were your exact words, weren't they, Peter?

PETER: Well, it's true. My mother died on the twenty-first of July 2004. Deevo Russell died on the nineteenth of July 2003. I don't see how this is relevant.

JOHN: You also told me something else: that after your mother died, you donated a substantial amount of money to the hospital. To the brilliant doctors who had done all they could to save her life.

PETER: Also quite true.

JOHN: (*looking around at everybody*) From this, ladies and gentlemen, I deduced that Harriet Landrigan *had not died instantly, after falling down the stairs.* If she had, she wouldn't have come into contact with any doctors. She'd have been taken to the morgue, not a hospital. I immediately thought to myself: she might have *died* on the twenty-first of July, but when did she have her so-called accident? A few days earlier, perhaps? Was it the nineteenth of July, Peter?

PETER: (*Slightly shocked*) Yes. Yes it was.

CLEM: That's exactly a year after Deevo died, to the very day. What a coincidence!

JOHN: I decided it was unlikely to be a coincidence. More likely was that someone – Mr E, perhaps – had violently pushed Harriet down the stairs on the first anniversary of Deevo Russell's death. Which led me to wonder: who would do that and why? Any thoughts, anybody? The answer's fairly obvious.

TESS: Well…Deevo Russell's decline began when Harriet refused to let him publish any more of her books. So maybe someone blamed her for his death and decided to punish her on its first anniversary.

JOHN: Exactly right! That's what happened. So, next question: who would care so passionately about avenging Deevo Russell's death that they might commit murder?

IRENE: (*accusingly, pointing her finger at MAX*) His son Max! It *must* be him! I've always thought there was something funny about Max, and I'm sure I'm not the only one.

MAX: Don't be silly, Irene. I was in this room with you when Swithun Kirk was stabbed. Mr Danes, please tell her…

JOHN: Max is innocent, Miss Coggins. Leave him alone.

MAX: Thank you.

JOHN: I, on the other hand, have a guilty conscience, and must make a confession. I took Harriet's unpublished books out of their frames and had a quick skim-read of them.

PETER: (*furious*) You did *what?*

JOHN: Don't worry. I had a little helper, who has already had them all reframed and with much better glass too – the kind used by the best museums and galleries. No damage has been done.

PETER: (*still furious*) This is outrageous!

CLEM: John, that's very naughty. Harriet *really* didn't want anyone to read those books. (*She leans in eagerly.*) Are they terribly scandalous and offensive?

JOHN: Not at all. They're completely inoffensive and quite ordinary-seeming romantic novels.

IRENE: How *dare* you? Nothing Harriet wrote was ordinary.

JOHN: The point is, there's nothing in any of the books that explains her refusal to publish them and to allow her fans to enjoy them. So the question then became…why was she so adamant that they must never be published? Any ideas?

OSCAR sticks his hand high in the air, as if at school.

JOHN: Yes, Oscar?

OSCAR: Maybe she wanted to hurt her publisher.

JOHN: (*rushes over to him eagerly*) Why do you say that?

OSCAR: (*surprised to be on the receiving end of so much positive attention*) Well, she carried on writing, didn't she? Those last four books got *written* – which means the only thing she stopped doing was publishing. And when she stopped publishing her novels, everyone was basically fine apart from Deevo. So maybe that was what she wanted – for him not to be fine. I mean, that's what happened, so it's possible that was all she wanted to happen. Maybe her only aim was to deprive him of the opportunity to publish her.

JOHN: Absolutely one hundred per cent correct, Oscar. You're an extremely talented boy, d'you know that?

ANDERS looks annoyed.

JOHN: (*to INSP C*) Oscar led me to a book in the library here called *The Mystery of Mr E*. It's a thriller by Deevo Russell, *who wrote books as well as publishing them* – remember that, Inspector. It's important. Inside *The Mystery of Mr E* I found, thanks to Oscar, the missing letters from the Russell, Russell & Russell archive – part of the correspondence between Harriet Landrigan and Deevo Russell – a crucial part. Do you want to hear some of the letters?

HARRIET and DEEVO appear at the front of the stage. Each of them is holding some letters.

HARRIET: (*reading from a letter*) Dear Deevo, All right, then, if you insist on knowing why I shall never again give you one of my books to publish, I'll tell you. As you might be aware, you yourself have recently written a book. You are now a writer as well as a publisher. No doubt, in your heart of hearts, you are a writer first and foremost. I trust you will require no further explanation. You should be able to work out the rest. Yours, Harriet.

DEEVO: (*reading from a letter*) Dear Harriet, What has my publishing a novel got to do with your books and your decision not to publish any more of them? You surely can't imagine that my doing a spot of writing will lessen my commitment to you and your work? Let me assure you that I remain as devoted to your novels and your career, and indeed to you, as I have always been. My publishing *The Mystery of Mr E* won't affect my work as your publisher at all – not one iota. I hope this solemn promise makes you feel better about things. Yours adoringly, Deevo.

HARRIET: (*reading from a letter*) Dear Deevo, No devoted publisher would compel his most valued author to accept a fellow author – some might even say a rival author – as her main ally and advocate in her writing life. Any sensible publisher would know that when he utters the words 'my books', his authors expect him to be referring to *their* books, which he loves as if they were his own – he believes in them, nurtures them, swells with pride when he thinks of them. As soon as the words 'my books' take on a different meaning for him – the books he has written, not the ones he publishes – then that publisher has, I'm afraid, lost the right to call himself devoted. I hope this clarifies things for you. Regards, Harriet.

DEEVO: (*reading from a letter*) Harriet, my dear, what on earth are you talking about? This is quite mad! Please tell me you're not threatening to move to another publisher! Yours most anxiously, Deevo.

HARRIET: (*reading from a letter*) Dear Deevo, No, you needn't worry. There will be no new publisher for me. I have just finished my latest novel, and no one will ever read it. I shall continue to write, of course. Writing is my greatest joy. But I shall never again publish a single word. Regards, Harriet.

DEEVO: (*reading from a letter*) Dear Harriet, I will not allow this to happen! You're being petty and pig-headed and plain stupid! You're making a tragedy out of something that needn't be a problem at all. I can't live without you or your books, and I don't believe you can live without me. You will miss me – you can't deny it. I will never stop begging you to change your mind. Yours desperately, Deevo.

HARRIET: (*looking at audience, stepping forward*) Dear Deevo…

SONG NO. 12: NO HAPPY ENDING

HARRIET sings:

You seem to imagine
That changing my mind
Would leave me with nothing to miss,
But if I stay here thinking you've robbed me blind
And wondering how it's come to this,
I'll still be stuck playing an unasked-for part
And taking up too hard a space in your heart,
And it might sound foolish
And it might sound foolish
But I wanted nothing to change.

DEEVO sings:

I'll never forget when you came to my door.

HARRIET sings:

You told me that I was the dream.

DEEVO sings:

I'd not met a young talent like you before.
We were an unbeatable team.

HARRIET sings:

Then you started playing a game of your own
And out of the blue came your claim to the throne
And it might sound foolish,
And it might sound strange,
But I wanted nothing to change.

I've no happy ending to offer you now,
Though I'll try to hope you succeed
In all your endeavours, if you will allow
That from now on, you'll never read
The stories I write that are so pure and free –
Designed to be pleasing to no one but me.
I'm proud to be foolish
And glad to be strange
And I now want nothing to change.

DEEVO sings:

For so many years, you've been my shining star.
How could you have failed to believe?
How can it be true that you've moved off too far –
A prize I can't hope to retrieve?
It's you who inspired me to dare to be more.

You were the dear reader I wrote my words for,
And it might sound foolish,
It might sound strange,
But I thought that nothing would change.

BOTH sing, in harmony, slowing down for end of song:

And it might sound foolish
And it might sound strange
But I wanted nothing to change.

JOHN: So you see, Harriet couldn't forgive Deevo for becoming a writer. To her, that was a betrayal of her and her books. I don't pretend to understand it. I'm not a creative type myself.

CLEM: Oh, I understand it! I think she's dead right. It's a huge conflict of interests.

PROF. T: You're surely not serious? Harriet and Deevo were writing in completely different genres – he was hardly a rival author. He was crime, she was romance.

TESS: I don't know. Presumably there's only one number one spot in the book charts?

JOHN: Harriet couldn't stop Deevo from writing and publishing his own novels, so she expressed her disapproval in the only way she could: by putting *her* books, all of her future work, beyond his reach.

TESS: Why didn't she just find a new publisher?

JOHN: I have a theory about that. She felt so betrayed by Deevo that preventing him from publishing her future books wasn't enough for her. She also wanted him to be unable to read them – and to know that, by writing and publishing his own novels, he had deprived the world of hers. I think she wanted him to believe he'd done a terrible thing.

PROF. T: Then – forgive me, Peter – but she must have been a silly, melodramatic and rather vain woman.

INSP C: Have I missed something? Have we been told yet who the murderer is?

SERG. W: We haven't been told that yet, boss. (*Checking his notes*) Unless I've missed it too...

INSP C: Get on with it, Mr Danes. Not all of us are fascinated by publishing world gossip, nor by the emotional intricacies of the author-publisher relationship. Who is the murderer? *Where* is the murderer?

JOHN: I'm getting there, Inspector. Max, tell us about the newly reinvented family publishing firm: Russell, Russell & Russell. There's you and your cousin Freddie, yes? That's two out of three. Tell me, what is the name of the third Russell family member currently running the company – your brother? I'll bet you everything I own that his first name begins with E.

MAX: (*stands up, shocked*) What...what are you saying?

JOHN: Who but a close relative of Deevo Russell would kill Harriet as payback for his death, and might have a first name that begins with E?

MAX: No. Not Edmund! I won't believe it.

JOHN: Edmund! So I'm right. (*Turns to INSP C*) Oscar told me that Deevo Russell built the library here at Idlewyld House while all its residents – the Landrigan family and Anders – were away on holiday. That means Deevo must have had a key to the house. I asked myself: what if that key was still in his possession when he died, and what if his son, Mr E, found it? Remember, Clemency Landrigan heard the front door being locked when the murderer left the house after killing Swithun Kirk. Realistically, how could the killer be anyone other than the Russell brother whose first name begins with E? That was my thinking. I suppose I could be wrong… (*He looks doubtful suddenly*) It might be pure coincidence that Max's brother's name is Edmund…

PROF. T: (*stands up and walks over to JOHN's side*) I don't think you're wrong, John. Max Russell was the only one of us guests who knew you would be here. Peter, you told him, didn't you? You mentioned to Max that he might one day persuade John to write his memoirs: 'Case Notes of a Generalist', or some such.

MAX: That's a fabulous title.

PROF. T: If Max knew in advance that John was coming here and if he was excited about a prospective book, he might have mentioned it to his brother and business partner Edmund Russell. Remember, Mr E knew when he went to John's house that John was coming here…

Enter MR E with a flourish

MR E: Well done, John Danes. Correct on all fronts. I am Edmund Russell. Otherwise known as 'the murderer', and also, of course, known as Mr E.

SERG W: (*to INSP C, with a nudge*) We've just found out who the murderer is, boss.

IRENE: (*stands, fist clenched and raised, says to MR E*) If only I had a knife in my hand – I'd stab you to death!

MR E: Oh, do feel free. Years in prison will be terribly dull, I expect. Death would be preferable.

OSCAR: My French teacher, Mrs Lapp, would agree with you. She's a big fan of executing people. She often mentions it during jury selection.

CLEM: Jury selection?

OSCAR: That's what she calls taking the register.

CLEMENCY sighs heavily.

JOHN: (*to MR E*) I don't understand you.

MR E: (*surprised*) Yes, you do. You've just explained it all to them. Strong desire to avenge death of tragically deceased father. Etcetera, etcetera.

JOHN: Yes, I understand that part. What I can't work out is why you'd come and introduce yourself to me as the guilty party, give me the first letter of your name… All right, so you didn't tell me which murder you'd committed, but you did challenge me to catch you, and you mentioned Idlewyld House. You must have known I'd poke around here until I found a murder. And then you killed Swithun Kirk, thinking he was me, because you feared I was onto you, I suppose. But I mean…the first person to put me onto you was…you.

MR E: Oh dear. You understand so little. How disappointing.

OSCAR: (*to JOHN*) I think he wanted to get caught.

MR E: Clever boy! At first, I wanted to get away with killing Harriet, and I did. I was pleased with myself…for a while. I stole the most revealing letters from the company archive. Anyone who read the cruel words Harriet wrote to my father would have realised I had a powerful motive, so I made those words disappear. Then it started to bother me that my great achievement – a successful murder – had gone unnoticed. If years pass and one gets no credit for one's hard work and ingenuity…well, it's pretty galling. So eventually I thought to myself, what if I were to turn it into a game? Find a likely opponent and set him a challenge: tell him I've murdered someone, but tell him no more than that. Mr Danes, I did not kill Swithun Kirk thinking he was you. His posture was quite different from yours; I'd never have mixed the two of you up. No, I killed him because I knew you weren't going to catch me unless I gave you some extra help. I didn't want to win too easily. Where's the fun in that? So I committed a second murder, right under your nose. That provided you with another helpful clue: that the killer must have had a key to Idlewyld House. You were immediately convinced that the second murder was committed to cover up the first, when in fact the opposite was true. The second murder was committed because, without it, you'd have allowed yourself to be persuaded that Harriet's death was a tragic accident.

JOHN: (*to MR E*) So Swithun Kirk dressing up in my hat and coat was a stroke of luck for you.

MR E: Yes. I let myself into the house intending to kill a random guest – or possibly Anders – just to make sure you were in no doubt that there was a murderer to be caught. When I saw Mr Kirk dressed in your clothes, I thought, 'How perfect!' I knew you'd assume I was trying to kill *you.*

INSP C: (*handcuffing him*) Come on, Mr E the murderer – it's jail time for you, and plenty of it.

MR E: (*Still talking to JOHN*) And now I am doomed to live out the rest of my days in a confined space – like one of Harriet Landrigan's last four novels. Except that *I* haven't been framed! I say, that's rather good, isn't it?

The police lead him away in handcuffs.

SCENE 7

Pffisham School – another prize giving. Large group scene. Present are: MR FRIEND, GWEN LAPP, MR MORRISON, MISS NEARY, OSCAR LANDRIGAN, BARTIE VOSS, CORNELIA VAN ZUYLEN, ASBO, JOHN DANES, PROF LAURA TAYLOR, CLEMENCY LANDRIGAN, PETER LANDRIGAN, FRANK VOSS, PAMOLYN VOSS.

MR FRIEND: And the Outstanding Achievement Award goes to… Oscar Landrigan, for services to justice.

MR FRIEND hands OSCAR a certificate. CLEMENCY, PETER, PROF TAYLOR and JOHN DANES all applaud. BARTIE VOSS cheers. PAMOLYN and FRANK VOSS look utterly devastated. Applause dies down.

BARTIE: (*shouting*) Bloody well done, Oscar!

MRS LAPP: (*stands up, addresses MR FRIEND*) Justice? *Justice*? I object, Your Honour. You cannot give a prize to a boy who never hands in his French homework! Oscar Landrigan, unless you present your overdue homework to me *right now*, you cannot receive your award. Now, where is your homework?

OSCAR: I refuse to answer, Miss, on the grounds that it might incriminate me.

MRS LAPP: Objection – argumentative!

MR FRIEND: Overruled, Mrs Lapp. (*He takes certificate back from her and hands it to OSCAR again.*) Oscar's helped to solve two murders. As someone who…pretends to be a legal professional, you of all people ought to agree that's an outstanding achievement. And now I hope you'll all join me in singing the Pffisham School Song.

MR FRIEND starts to sing:

Ita erat quando hic adveni…

BARTIE: Actually, sir…

MR FRIEND: Yes, Bartie?

BARTIE: Oscar and I have written a new school song. We were wondering whether we might…

OSCAR: Ditch the old, boring one.

MRS LAPP: (*indignantly*) There's nothing wrong with the school song.

OSCAR: There is, though? It's seventeen minutes long, most of it's in Latin, and it's the subject of an ongoing internet hate campaign.

MRS LAPP: (*to MR FRIEND*) Your Honour – I urge you to be *not at all* lenient with these boys. Nobody gave them permission to write a song!

BARTIE: Why don't we let Mr. Friend decide which one he prefers, Mrs Lapp? (*Sidling up to MR FRIEND with an ingratiating smile and a small deferential bow*) He is, after all, our esteemed headmaster. Sir, would you like to have a go at singing our new song? Oscar and I are rather proud of our little collaboration.

MR FRIEND: Give it here, then.

BARTIE hands him the lyrics.

SONG NO. 13: THE PFFISHAMIAN SONG (GATES OF GOLD)

MR FRIEND sings:

The Pffishamian way
Is as awesome today
As it was when our first gates of gold
Opened up to bestow
Everything that we know
On the young and the not hugely old...

PETER: (*to JOHN*) I feel churlish bringing this up when you've done so well solving two murders, John, but...you had no damn right to break into those frames and read my mother's books. And you haven't succeeded at the task I assigned you.

JOHN: You mean removing all your house guests and deterring them from ever pestering you again? No, I haven't, have I? Ah well, if it makes you feel any better, I firmly intend to remove at least one of them before the day is out.

PETER: You do?

JOHN: Yes! (*He points to PROF TAYLOR*). Laura. I'm going to ask her to marry me. With any luck, that will lead to her hanging around my house from now on, not yours.

PROF. T: I shall actually be rather busy hanging around my office at the university. I've had a brilliant idea for a new research project. It's about publishers who are also authors and the effect that has had on literature. The wedding will have to wait.

JOHN: (*to PETER*) I think that's her way of saying she would be delighted to marry me, Peter. Hardly the most romantic way to put it, but it's better than nothing, I suppose.

PROF. T: (*defensively*) It was hardly the most romantic proposal. You didn't even address me directly!

CLEM: I'm confused. Are you two getting married or not?

PROF & JD: (*crossly, in unison*) Yes.

PETER: (*distracted; vaguely pleased but still a bit worried*) Oh… well, that's lovely news. Lovely news.

JOHN: As for your other guests, I've got an idea: why don't we ask Mr Friend to give them all jobs here? That'll keep them too busy to bother you. Max can teach Creative Writing, as well as running his firm with cousin Freddie. As a book industry expert, he'll be invaluable, I'm sure. Tess Yolland can teach art. And Irene Coggins can teach Gwen Lapp how to teach French.

PETER: Does Irene speak French?

JOHN: Think about it, Peter. She'll have made a point of reading your mother's books in every language they've been translated into. In order to do that, she'll have had to learn those languages first.

MR FRIEND sings:

The Pffishamian style
Is to bear with a smile
All the adversities that unfold.

We have strong discipline
But we let kids stay in
Over lunch break if it's really cold.

MR FRIEND, MISS NEARY, MR MORRISON and MRS LAPP sing:

Though we've moved several times
Our old school bell still chimes
And our talents, they are manifold.
It's not you, it's not me,
It's our community
And our ethos of breaking the mold.

MR FRIEND sings:

So whatever you do
Just be proud to be you,
And remember, when strict parents scold,
You've been pupils of mine,
So you'll end up just fine
Even if you're not Oxbridge-enrolled.

ALL sing:

The Pffishamian song
Once went on far too long,
And we were, on the internet, trolled.
This new song's the right length;
We go from strength to strength.

MR FRIEND sings:

We're Pffishamians,

ALL sing:

We're Pffishamians…

MR FRIEND sings:

A Pffishamian….always has hands to hold.

ALL sing:

We're Pffishamians,
We're Pffisha-mi-ans,
We're Pffishamians… of whom great tales are told!

THE END

WORK EXPERIENCE

A musical locked-room mystery

Book, all lyrics and some tunes by Sophie Hannah

Music by Annette Armitage

This musical was performed by the pupils of Sancton Wood School in Cambridge in 2018.

Newspaper headline board-holder 1
Newspaper headline board-holder 2
Other newspaper board-holders

***

Narrator

***

Police

Inspector Coode, Sergeant Wilderspin

The Surridge Family

Derek Surridge – managing director of Tribute Adhesive Gel Solutions (TAGS)
Eve Surridge – Derek's ex-wife
Luke Surridge – Derek's missing son
Diane Surridge – Derek's sister
Duncan Surridge – Derek's brother

***

Richard Magnus – Derek Surridge's lawyer

***

Karen Beaton – true crime podcaster

***

TAGS employees

Cathy
Jen
Annie
Grace
Leo
Molly
Paul

***

The Landrigan Family – and friends

Oscar Landrigan – a pupil at Pffisham School

Peter Landrigan – Oscar's father, and son of the late Harriet Landrigan, the bestselling romantic novelist of all time

Clemency Landrigan – Oscar's mother, a perfume designer

Oscar's gang of mates, the Reprobates: Tobias Boland (ASBO), Waspy, 3-Strike

The Voss Family

Bartie Voss – Pffisham School's star pupil
Bethany Voss – Bartie's sister and Oscar Landrigan's girlfriend
Frank and Pamolyn Voss – parents of Bartie and Bethany
Fred Croft – The Vosses' neighbour, and Bethany's boyfriend when she's trying to make Oscar jealous

Pffisham School Staff, Prefects and Students

Mrs Gwen Lapp – head teacher of Pffisham School, formerly teacher of French, even though she couldn't speak French
Mr Morrison – teacher of History
Miss Neary – teacher of Music
Miss Windsor – teacher of English
Monsieur LeClay – a fake model of a French teacher, made of clay
Natalia (prefect)
Isaac (prefect)
Kate (prefect)

County Council Staff

Lynda Terry – head of work experience placements for the council, and the force behind a new county-wide scheme to improve the behaviour of teenage boys

The Wrongly Accused

George
Henry
Danny
Wendy
Serena

The Advice Seekers

Lizzie
Izzy
Gina
Zena
Bill
Simon

Camera Crew, journalists

SONGS/MUSICAL NUMBERS

ACT ONE:

Overture
Everywhere I'd Rather Be
The Day of the Terrible Boy
Windows All Locked Firmly
Work Experi-ness
So Long, Gone
Find You (original)
Can We Drug You?
It Dawned on Me
You Remind Me of Someone

ACT TWO:

I'm Sure We Can All Agree
Dear Stand-up Ashtray
Something Can Be Done
Ballad of the Wrongly Accused
If I Cut My Finger
That Works For Me
Here's To You, Gavin Williamson
Son-in-Law
Find You (Oscar's Edit)
Enemy Avenue
The Day of the Wonderful Boy
Let's Pretend to be Heroes

ACT ONE

SCENE 1

Enter two newspaper-board holders, while Overture plays, holding up signs to cover their faces. Each sign bears a photo of LUKE SURRIDGE'S face and an article about LUKE with headlines as per below:

NBH 1: 13-year-old Luke Surridge disappears from locked room at secondary school. Police are questioning his father, Derek Surridge. Sources say the arrest of Mr Surridge is imminent.

While overture is still playing, lots of newspaper board-holders, all with articles on their boards from different years, walk across the stage one by one, muttering 'No developments in the case of the lost schoolboy…' and 'Police say they're still stumped in the puzzling case of…' and 'Case goes cold, as local boy remains missing…' and 'Ten months after he vanished, police appeal for any witnesses who might not have come forward when school pupil disappeared from…' We get the sense that time is passing, and no progress is being made.

NBH 2: Latest in disappearance of local teenager Luke Surridge, who has been at the centre of a baffling mystery since he disappeared from a locked room last year. All charges against Luke's father, Derek Surridge, for the kidnap and murder of his son have been dropped. Police are no closer to finding Luke Surridge.

Overture fades out.

Board-holders, keeping their faces covered by their signs, take a step back and stand in a line at the back of the stage as NARRATOR walks on, holding a newspaper. Enter INSPECTOR COODE and RICHARD MAGNUS. They stand on either side of NARRATOR as he reads aloud to the audience from a newspaper:

NARR: 16th of September. Derek Surridge has today been released from police custody, and all charges against him in connection with the disappearance of his now-14-year-old son Luke have been dropped. Luke Surridge disappeared from his school on September the 9th last year, and, twelve months later, he has still not been found. His father Derek, a 47-year-old GP, was arrested by Cambridgeshire police following Luke's disappearance, after a witness reported seeing a man fitting Mr Surridge's description behaving suspiciously in close proximity to Luke's school on the day the teenager disappeared. However, after conducting a thorough investigation, police concluded that there was insufficient evidence to prosecute Mr Surridge for any criminal offence. Detective Inspector Oliver Coode of Cambridgeshire Police said...

INSP C: We have not given up. We will continue to search for Luke Surridge, as we continue to investigate all unsolved missing persons cases. By applying the ever-evolving methods of modern policing, we are confident we will one day find the answers that have eluded us so far.

NARR: Speaking for Derek Surridge, solicitor Richard Magnus said...

RICH M: My client is relieved that his legal ordeal is over, though his personal anguish will continue for as long as his son Luke remains missing. In addition to the loss of his son, he has also had to endure a heartbreaking separation from his wife, who initiated divorce proceedings against him after police first expressed an interest in questioning him, on the grounds that...

NB1 throws her sign into the wings, walks forward with a harsh, cold expression on her face and becomes a new character, EVE SURRIDGE.

EVE SURR: (*nastily*) There's no smoke without fire.

RICH M: …and who subsequently won sole custody of Luke, should he ever be found alive and well. We intend to appeal this ludicrous judgement – for the simple reason that if Luke Surridge were to be found safe and well, he would also be able to confirm that his father had neither abducted nor killed him. There would therefore be no reason not to award joint custody to Derek Surridge and his soon-to-be-ex wife.

EVE SURRIDGE huffs and makes a grumpy, resentful face at RICHARD MAGNUS.

RICH M: Finally, my client has a personal message for the police, which he has asked me to convey: (*He moves to the front and centre of the stage.*) 'Dear Cambridgeshire Police: I am writing to beg you to remove Inspector Oliver Coode from the investigation into my son's disappearance. It is nothing short of scandalous that in the past twelve months he has failed to gain access to the locked classroom from which Luke disappeared. His claim that he has been refused entry to the school because he lacks the required visitor pass in a plastic wallet, and that the school is currently short-staffed and so unable to furnish him with said pass, is feeble in the extreme. Please replace this buffoon with a more able Detective Inspector at your earliest convenience. Yours in hope, Derek Surridge.'

NARR: Karen Beaton, host of the 'Justice for Locked Room Luke' podcast, and founder of the website of the same name, said…

NB2 throws her sign into the wings, walks forward with a harsh, cold expression on her face and becomes a new character, KAREN BEATON.

KAREN B: I have no words to describe my horror at this latest development: the release of Derek Surridge, who, as we all know, is highly likely to be a murderer, and who has been inconsiderately protesting his innocence for a whole year, knowing full well that I and my many thousands of podcast subscribers believe him to be guilty of…(*a hesitant look appears on her face, then she ploughs on determinedly*) whatever it was that happened that day. There's no doubt that something sinister occurred, and I'm confident that Derek Surridge was responsible for it, whatever it was. I'm delighted to hear that he's had to shut down his GP practice after all his patients signed a petition saying they would rather die of appendicitis than ever be treated by him again. At least that's some small measure of justice.

ALL exit apart from NARRATOR, who stays on stage, as set for new scene assembles around him.

SCENE 2

TAGS offices. Big sign on wall says, 'Welcome to Tribute Adhesive Gel Solutions (TAGS) Ltd'. Desks and chairs are all over the stage, many desks have old fashioned telephones on them.

NARR: 23rd of February, two years later.

Exit NARRATOR.

Enter CATHY and JEN. They're wearing jackets and have handbags over their shoulders. They take off their jackets and drape them over the chairs. Then they put their bags on or over the chairs too. They stand and look around, slightly awe-struck and nervous. Neither one acknowledges the other's presence. They eye each other cautiously, then quickly look away, too scared to make eye-contact.

Enter TAGS STAFF, holding files and papers. Each one dances across the stage, paying no attention to CATHY and JEN, singing excitedly…

ANNIE: It's the day, it's the day… *(exits)*

MOLLY: It's the day, it's the day… *(exits)*

GRACE: Hip hooray, it's the day, it's the day… *(exits)*

LEO: It's today, it's the day… *(exits)*

CATHY: (*to JEN, timidly, no social skills, painfully shy*) Excuse me? Sorry. Excuse me?

JEN: (*turns, timidly, also no social skills*) Oh, sorry. Er…hello?

CATHY: I'm just wondering if I'm in the right place? Is this TAGS? Tribute Adhesive Gel Solutions?

JEN: I hope so, or else I'm in the wrong place too. (*She points to the large sign on the wall*). The sign does say 'Tribute Adhesive Gel Solutions...'

CATHY: I know. But TAGS is supposed to be a workplace that offers neither excitement nor fun. And...four people who looked as if they work here just danced past, and they were *singing*. They seemed to be having quite a lot of fun. And did you hear *what* they were singing? 'Hip hooray'? I'm not sure that's the sort of working environment I'm looking for.

JEN: Me neither. I was expecting the offices to be silent, and all the staff to be timid and unremarkable, like me.

CATHY: So...are you here for the job interview too? (*Faces audience, obviously panicking*) Oh, no! This is awful! One of us is going to get the job and the other isn't. What if I get it and she hates me? What if she gets it and I hate her? I can't cope with this.

JEN: (*walking over to CATHY*) Don't worry. We're not in competition with each other. Haven't you looked at the company website?

CATHY: No. I was too scared to switch on my laptop, in case it overheated and exploded.

JEN: I looked – only for two minutes, in case the electromagnetic waves from the WiFi prompted my vital organs to shut down – but I saw something very reassuring. On the home page it says in capital letters: 'Tribute Adhesive Gel Solutions: anyone who wants to work here, can.'

CATHY: Oh, that's such a relief! I'm still concerned about the singing people, though. I hope they don't sing regularly.

JEN: Why do you think they were singing, 'It's the day, it's today'? At TAGS, every day is supposed to be the same: dull, predictable, routine.

CATHY: Yes, that's what the job advert said: no holidays or days off, ever – so one never has to worry about how to fill uncomfortable moments of… (*lowers her voice, as if she's about to say something shocking*)…free time.

Both CATHY and JEN wince and shudder in disgust at the idea of free time.

CATHY: It sounds like the dream job. Don't you think?

JEN: I suppose so.

CATHY: Look, they've even got old-fashioned telephones, so that we can pretend we're still living in the good old days when everything was lovely.

JEN: (*doubtfully*) I do definitely want to feel secure and protected. It's just, sometimes I wonder whether maybe…

CATHY: (*stern, wanting to shut her down*) What? You shouldn't wonder. I don't allow myself to wonder about anything. Ever.

JEN: You're right. We're much better off here than anywhere else.

SONG NO. 1: EVERYWHERE I'D RATHER BE

JEN sings:

Most people don't know what life has in store for them.
If they are lucky, they'll fall on their feet,
Wishing and dreaming that there could be more for them
Than they can see from the end of their street.
Taking their chances, they hope if they've tried their best
Everything good will be coming their way.
No guarantees, even if they can pass the test –
Some have to lose at the games we all play…

JEN and CATHY sing:

I'd rather know for sure
What each day has in store:
These desks and chairs and phones –
No risks, and no unknowns.
That's why, as long as I'm alive,
From half past nine to half past five
You'll find me here, day in, day out,
Trying so hard not to think about…

(Enter ANNIE, GRACE, LEO and MOLLY. They stand behind JEN and CATHY)

JEN and CATHY sing:

A cruise to some Norwegian fjord
With rich celebrities on board.
Though these four walls are all I see,
There's everywhere I'd rather be.
The Colca Canyon in Peru,
A quiet tree-lined avenue,

Somewhere near Washington DC.
There's everywhere I'd rather be.

JEN, CATHY, ANNIE, GRACE, LEO and MOLLY sing:

A crowded bench in Central Park,
The Eiffel Tower after dark,
The Taj Mahal, Stone Henge, Times Square.
Just think – I could be anywhere.
I'll never see the Philippines
Except in travel magazines.
I don't know where Niagara Falls.
All day I sit here taking calls –

JEN sings:

Reliable, polite and clear,
Day after day, year after year,
And though I need the certainty,
There's everywhere I'd rather be –

CATHY sings:

The Pyramids. The Parthenon.
I could go now… I haven't gone.

JEN and CATHY sing:

You wouldn't think to look at me,
There's everywhere I'd rather be.

ALL sing:

A desert, forest, mountain range –
All out of reach. Will something change?

Will someone look my way and see
There's everywhere I'd rather be?

Enter DIANE SURRIDGE and DUNCAN SURRIDGE, with PAUL trailing in behind them. PAUL goes to stand beside ANNIE, GRACE, MOLLY and LEO.

DIANE: Aha! You must be Cathy and Jennifer – here for your job interviews – correct?

CATHY: Yes.

JEN: That's right.

DIANE: Congratulations – you've both got the job! I'm Diane Surridge. This is my brother, Duncan Surridge. I'm the Deputy Managing Director.

DUNCAN: And I'm the Deputy Deputy Managing Director. Welcome to Tribute Adhesive Gel Solutions. We all call it TAGS. I invite you to do the same.

DIANE: Especially when you need a rhyme for a song. Lots of things rhyme with TAGS. Bags, flags…

CATHY: (*scared*) A song? But…I thought it was supposed to be boring here. I can't work in a place where there's singing.

JEN: I agree with Cathy. It's not what we were expecting at all.

DUNCAN: That's rather hypocritical, don't you think? You two were both singing, only a moment ago.

JEN: (*indignantly*) No, we weren't.

CATHY: We were expressing our innermost thoughts. If they happened to take the form of an 'I want' song in a musical, we can hardly be blamed for that. It certainly doesn't mean we were singing. We weren't.

DUNCAN: Well…that's either an interesting interpretation or a lie. Let's say it's a lie. (*Looks around eagerly, asks everyone*) What happens to liars, here at TAGS?

PAUL: They don't get fired!

DIANE: (*beaming*) That's correct. Nobody here gets fired, or retired. You'll be working weekdays and weekends, and there are no holidays.

DUNCAN: You will be paid very well, provided with nice stodgy spice-free lunches every day for the rest of your lives, and comfortable office furniture to sit on. There will be no change, career advancement, excitement or fun from the day you start until…well, until your last day – ahem – and there will also be no unpleasantness, no conflict, no terrible days at work. And certainly no simmering resentment or feuds with colleagues, nothing like that. Our employees are far too conflict-averse.

DIANE: Here at TAGS, we pride ourselves on ensuring that every day is exactly the same.

DUNCAN: The managing director, Derek Surridge…he's our brother, in case you were wondering why we all share a surname. And he's passionate about providing a lifetime of uneventful predictability for all of his staff. He believes that joy and fulfilment are illusory goals, and that the only true route to inner peace is via the monotony of the humdrum. That is what he provides here at TAGS.

CATHY: Excuse me. I'm sorry to interrupt, but… Jennifer and I saw some TAGS employees looking and sounding quite excited a few minutes ago. Those ones over there. (*She points.*) They were singing 'Hip hooray, it's today!'

DIANE: Yes, I was coming to that. Have you heard of Pffisham School? The enormous grey stone building with lots of turrets and towers, in the grounds of Idelwyld House? It's Cambridge's least successful and also most expensive private school.

JEN: Yes, I think I've heard of it. Isn't that…?

CATHY: Yes, it is. I read about it in *The Times*.

DIANE: I'm sure you did. Pffisham is the school that got into trouble for pretending that a large clay model of a middle-aged man was the new French teacher.

DUNCAN: Parents raised the alarm after their children told them Monsieur LeClay never spoke or moved during lessons.

DIANE: Mr Surridge, our managing director, has a…well, let's call it a special connection with that particular school. Each year, he offers a week's work experience at TAGS to Pffisham School's most disobedient and uncontrollable pupil.

JEN: Why does he do that? If he wants life at TAGS to be dull and predictable…

CATHY: I suppose he'll explain when we meet him.

DIANE: You are unlikely to meet Mr Surridge. These days, he… well, he rather dreads coming into contact with his fellow humans. He tends to stay in his office on the fourth floor. Hasn't ventured out for more than a year. Any messages he wishes to deliver will be conveyed by me or Duncan. And…if you happen to catch a glimpse at the end of a corridor of a man dressed in pyjamas, dressing gown and slippers, do not approach him, please. Mr Surridge hates to be unexpectedly approached.

DUNCAN: (*to JEN*) In answer to your question, Jennifer… Mr Surridge is a very kind man. He believes in giving people a chance. That's why every year, he offers this amazing work experience opportunity to Pffisham School's most terrible boy. So far, the worst pupil of the year has always been a boy.

DIANE: All our staff get rather excited on the day that the new Terrible Boy is due to arrive. It's the only interesting thing that ever happens here. This worried Mr Surridge at first – as I've explained, he's firmly opposed to excitement – but one has to strike a balance, and in the end he decided that one week of novelty and drama each year couldn't do too much harm.

DUNCAN: If anything, it makes us appreciate the tedium of the rest of our year all the more.

General murmur of agreement from DIANE and TAGS STAFF.

LEO: (*excited*) And today's the day! The new Terrible Boy is arriving at 2 o'clock this afternoon!

SONG NO. 2: THE DAY OF THE TERRIBLE BOY

ALL apart from JEN and CATHY sing:

It's the day,
It's the day,
Only day of the year we enjoy!
So we say
Hip hooray,
It's the day of the terrible boy!

MOLLY sings:

Will he swear, will he smell,
Cast a horrible spell?
Will he hot-wire or bug Mr Surridge's car?
Will he break someone's arm
Or set off the alarm?
We can't wait.

LEO shouts:

We can't wait!

ALL sing:

Oh how lucky we are!

It's the day,
It's the day,
Only day of the year we enjoy!
So we say
Hip hooray,
It's the day of the terrible boy!

ANNIE sings:

We had fun with the one
Who came in with a gun
And shot out all the bulbs of the lights on our floor.
We enjoyed one called Lloyd
Who arrived and destroyed
Mr Surridge's printer, then kicked down the door.

ALL, including JEN and CATHY, sing:

Just today
There's a way
To have fun. It's excitement ahoy!
Time to play!
It's the day,
It's the day of the terrible boy.
Hip hooray,
It's the day,
It's the day of the terrible boy!

Lights go down.

SCENE 3

Pffisham School, Art Classroom. OSCAR LANDRIGAN, WASPY and 3-STRIKE are all looking at a piece of paper on which there is a complicated drawing that looks like an architect's plan for a large building.

OSCAR: Right, guys, listen. These are the original architect's drawings for Pffisham School. If you look carefully, you'll see that there's a gap just there (*he points*) between the ground floor and the basement. It looks like some kind of cavity, and it runs from one end of the building to the other. And here, up the side of the building, there's another large gap – and this one's vertical. If these drawings are accurate, it goes all the way up to the Detention Unit on the second floor.

WASPY: Where did you get these drawings? Did you steal them?

OSCAR: Course not. I'm not that stupid. If the drawings went missing, the teachers might guess that I'm planning to break ASBO out of the Unit.

3-STRIKE: Then where does this drawing come from?

OSCAR: I did it myself. After sneaking a look at the plans and memorising them.

WASPY: No way!

OSCAR: I did. It took me nine full days, and that was working at top speed. ASBO's not going to last much longer in the Detention Unit, in complete isolation. He's only lasted this long because I've promised to buy him a brand new iPhone soon as we've broken him out. I told him, just keep thinking to yourself: 'New iPhone, new iPhone.' ASBO's tough. I don't *think* he'll crack, but we can't afford to take too long. So look, all we need to do is find a way in on that side of the building. Then we can just crawl along a bit and…

GWEN LAPP, head teacher, enters. She peers at the drawing over Oscar's shoulder.

GWEN L: Is that your handiwork, Oscar Landrigan?

OSCAR: Yes, miss. It's good, isn't it? It's, um…it's my art project for this term.

GWEN L: Personally, I wouldn't hang it on my wall, but…well, I've noticed how hard you've been working on it and I have to say, I'm impressed. You've shown real dedication and artistic commitment. Staying at school overnight, missing all your lunch breaks…You haven't complained once about all the hard slog and effort involved. (*With a knowing smile*) I think I can guess why the sudden change in attitude.

OSCAR: (*worried, under his breath to his friends*) Shit. (*Turns to GWEN LAPP*) I mean…surely not, Miss?

GWEN L: Oh, yes, I think so. I believe you and a certain person have recently become "an item", as you youngsters like to say?

OSCAR: No one under fifty would say that but…yeah, I suppose me and Bethany are sort of –

GWEN L: Not 'Me and Bethany'. 'Bethany and *I*.' (*Turns her attention back to the drawing*) Now, I have one question. (*She points*) What is it?

OSCAR: Oh, um…(*thinks quickly*) It's called, er 'Interactions and… Refractions'. The lines represent the, er…socio-psychological terrain of the contemporary teenager.

GWEN L: (*impressed*) That's extremely clever.

OSCAR: Thanks, Miss. Since I'm in your good books at the moment, might I ask a favour?

GWEN L: That depends what it is.

OSCAR: It's ASBO. Sentencing him to isolation in the Detention Unit for eleven months is incredibly unfair, especially –

GWEN L: Silence at once! He's a vile reprobate and must remain locked away for as long as I loathe him as much as I presently do.

OSCAR: But he's done nothing wrong! And you used to loathe me too, remember?

GWEN L: Yes, but *you*, dear Oscar, are now dating the lovely Bethany, sister of our star pupil, Bartie Voss. That changes everything.

OSCAR: I'm not sure I am…*(looks dubious about saying the word, makes air quotes with his fingers)* "dating" her any more. To be honest, she's been acting a bit off lately.

GWEN L: Nonsense! Bethany's behaviour is always exemplary. I'm firmly on her side, even knowing nothing about what has occurred. Don't argue with me, Oscar. Leave your art project for now and go to reception at once.

OSCAR: Why?

GWEN L: (*gathers herself*) There's an important visitor here to see you – from the County Council. And your mother, too.

OSCAR: Mum? What's she doing here?

GWEN L: They're both waiting, so run along. And I don't want to hear another word about freeing Tobias Boland – or ASBO, as you insist on calling him – from his richly-deserved captivity. The Detention Unit is exactly where that miscreant belongs.

Exit GWEN LAPP. OSCAR exits in the opposite direction, with a sigh.

SCENE 4

Detention Unit, Pffisham School. ASBO is alone in the room, with only a table and a chair there. He's banging on the wall.

ASBO: Let me out! I haven't done anything wrong! (*He sits down on a chair, starts muttering to himself determinedly…*) New iPhone, new iPhone. (*He stands and walks to the front of the stage.*) I didn't even pick up that pencil case, let alone throw it at anyone. I've been stitched up!

SONG NO. 3: WINDOWS ALL LOCKED FIRMLY

ASBO sings:

Windows all locked firmly.
Stuck here till January.
No crisps, no chocolate –
So brutal. So cruel.

No chance of jokes or chat.
Stuck here just thinking that
Actual prison
Might be more fun than school.

I did not flip my pencil case
Or throw it at Gwen Lapp's face.
If she says I did, then she's told you a lie.

Windows all locked firmly,
Heightened security.
They think they'll crush me
But they're doomed to fail

For if you mess with Reprobates,
You'll be hearing from their mates.
The best friends of Oscar
Will always prevail.

MR MORRISON enters with some green chicken on a tray.

Don't bring me a lunch tray!
Not from the canteen.
I swear, I'm not guilty.
That chicken is green.

MR MORRISON puts the green chicken down on the table, on its tray, and then leaves the room.

ASBO sings:

Windows all locked firmly.

ASBO sweeps the chicken off the table, onto the floor.

Get that away from me!
Best friends of Oscar
Are never alone,
So expel me today
And I'll cheer all the way
For I have been promised a brand new iPhone.

Lights go down.

SCENE 5

Reception, Pffisham School. LYNDA TERRY and CLEMENCY LANDRIGAN are talking. They are both seated. LYNDA is holding some papers.

LYNDA: This is a wonderful opportunity for Oscar, Mrs Landrigan. He's very lucky. TAGS employees consistently report a higher level of contentment than those who work for nearly all other local businesses. Oscar's all set to have an extremely rewarding week!

OSCAR enters.

LYNDA: Hello, Oscar! How lovely to meet you. I'm Lynda Terry, from the County Council. I'm in charge of organising work exper-iness placements for Cambridgeshire.

OSCAR: Work what?

LYNDA: Work experi-ness.

CLEM: She means work experience. Despite being in charge of it, she's unable to pronounce it.

OSCAR: Mum, what's going on?

CLEM: I'm afraid I have some upsetting news, darling. The County Council has decided to send you to some wretched glue-making establishment. I've no idea why.

OSCAR: (*disconsolately*) I don't want to make glue.

LYNDA: Don't be silly, Oscar. It'll be huge fun! Derek Surridge, TAGS's managing director, is absolutely determined that we should send him the worst pupil from Pffisham School every year for a week's work experi-ness. (*Turns to CLEM*) I've done my research, Mrs Landrigan, and there's no doubt that Oscar is the most unmanageable pupil this year.

OSCAR looks proud, nodding and grinning.

CLEM: That's absolute rubbish! Isn't it, Oscar?

OSCAR: (*debonair, charming, with a smile*) Is it?

LYNDA: Additionally, Oscar has repeatedly declined to take part in the council's new 'Yuck! Boys!' initiative – specifically designed for the improvement of appalling boys from a wide range of diverse and underrepresented backgrounds. It's such a shame he doesn't want to join in, especially since his particular demographic is…well, it's the most underrepresented that the County Council has ever had within its grasp. It would do wonders for our statistics if we could get him into the scheme.

CLEM: His 'particular demographic'? What on earth does that mean?

LYNDA: Immensely wealthy grandsons of famous murdered romantic novelists. Oscar is a minority of exactly nought-point-five. He's the only one of his…type in the whole county. It would be a huge coup for 'Yuck! Boys!' to get him.

CLEM: But…surely he must be a minority of one, since there's one of him?

LYNDA: Oh! (*Laughs fondly*) At the County Council we count each boy as a point-five. If he were a girl he'd count as one, of course. The trouble is, we can't count him at all, because he refuses to admit he's appalling and join 'Yuck! Boys!'. He wrote a letter to the council making the case that there is nothing wrong with him. According to Oscar, he is simply a… (*to OSCAR*) how did you put it?

OSCAR: A lovable free spirit, unsuited to the restrictions of childhood.

CLEM: That's exactly what he is. (*Springs to her feet.*) I'll tell you who's appalling: anyone who devises a programme to improve the behaviour of boys and calls it 'Yuck! Boys!'.

LYNDA: Oh, don't you like the name? We at the County Council think it has a pleasing ring to it. When it comes to dealing with boys, we find it's far better to be direct. Now, girls are a whole different ball game–

CLEM: Mrs Terry, I really don't want Oscar to be packed off to some adhesive gel company, and especially not now, when he's enjoying his school art project so much. He's been working on it day and night. Can't you send ASBO to do the work experience instead? He's a little bit worse than Oscar, isn't he?

LYNDA: (*checks her notes, frowns*) It does seem so, yes, but ASBO is unavailable at present, having recently been sentenced to eleven months in Pffisham's Detention Unit as a punishment for terribly bad behaviour.

OSCAR: (*indignantly*) ASBO's done nothing wrong.

LYNDA: Besides, Mrs Landrigan, you can hardly claim we're being unfair to Oscar. He did commit two murders last year, after all.

CLEM: (*whirls around, furious*) What?! No, he didn't. He helped to *solve* two murders!

LYNDA: (*looks confused*) Did he? Hold on, let me check. (*She looks at the papers she's holding.*) Yes, you're quite right. My mistake. He helped to solve two murders, that's true (*frowns, puzzled by what she's reading*) – as, er, sidekick to a man named John Danes, The Generalist. Still…(*she rallies, and looks determined and confident again*)…there's no denying that two murders occurred and that Oscar was involved.

CLEM: In the *solving* of them, yes. Which was a good thing. I trust the County Council understands the difference between a good thing and a bad thing?

LYNDA: Absolutely! Which is how I know it's going to be extremely beneficial for Oscar to have a nice bit of proper experi-ness in a lovely local business. Don't you think so, Oscar?

OSCAR: No. (*Resigned, sighing*) When's this happening?

LYNDA: Immediately. There's a car waiting outside to take us to TAGS now.

OSCAR: *What*? No way. I can't go now. I have to break ASBO out of… (*stops.*) I mean, I have to finish my amazing art project. (*Turns to CLEM*) Mum, I *cannot* go anywhere today, it's the worst possible time. Bethany will definitely dump me for good if I disappear without telling her. Can't you and Dad buy this TAGS place and, like, close it down before I get there?

CLEM: Not this week, darling. I'm launching my new fragrance in Paris on Wednesday, and then there's the Perfumiers' Conference in Milan… Mrs Terry, Oscar's grandmother left him more than enough money to sustain him in great comfort for the rest of his life. He doesn't need to experience what you…(*wrinkles nose in disgust*) job-having types call 'work' for a week, or even for half an hour. I'm three times his age and I have never worked, apart from for myself and in a creative capacity, and I'm quite all right. (*She puts on her best ingratiating smile*) I'm a perfume designer, you've probably heard of me: Clemency Landrigan. (*LYNDA shakes her head. CLEM looks disappointed. Then she brightens, having just had a thought that might save the day.*) Oh! And my friend Felicity who has a 'proper job' says it's perfectly dreadful! She's expected to go there *day after day*. I don't see why Oscar should have to experience that. It sounds horrid.

Three TEACHERS enter: MISS WINDSOR, MR MORRISON, MISS NEARY.

LYNDA: (*to TEACHERS*) Excuse me – do you work here, at Pffisham School?

MISS N: Yes. Why?

LYNDA: This parent, Mrs Landrigan, is being uncooperative.

MISS W: She's always uncooperative.

CLEM: That's not true. I mean…well, it *is* true. But the thing is… if you're interested, Mrs Terry?

LYNDA: (*brightly*) Not really! I just want to get my way, and then leave.

CLEM: A woman after my own heart! I am not *innately* disagreeable – only when the suggestions put before me are dreadful ones. Present me with a good idea and, I assure you, I shall greet it with paroxysms of glee.

LYNDA: (*thinking hard*) A good idea…let's see. Ooh, I've got one! I've always wanted to introduce massive parking fines for people who park in their own garages.

CLEM: (*scathing*) I'm sure you have. (*Shakes her head in disgust.*)

LYNDA: Now, listen, Mrs Landrigan: I've forgotten the earlier part of our conversation, so I'm no longer annoyed with you. Let's start afresh, shall we? Oscar will go and do his work experi-ness at TAGS and that's all there is to it!

MISS W: Yes, please let him go!

MR M: Please take him away!

MISS N: We've all been counting on a week of him being somewhere else.

LYNDA: (*crossly, remembering*) As for him never needing to work if he doesn't want to, well, bully for him! I have to spend most of my life working, and so do my colleagues. Most people do!

The TEACHERS gather round, behind LYNDA TERRY, as she starts to sing.

SONG NO. 4: WORK EXPERI-NESS

LYNDA TERRY sings:

Cartoonists, satirical,
Scientists, empirical –
All, by some miracle,
Work all day long.
Farmers, quite tractor-y,
Film stars, well actor-y,
Blokes in a factory,
Join in our song:

Work experi-ness,
Work experi-ness,
Monday to Friday, a whole week of weariness.
You'll learn why grown-ups aren't all full of cheeriness,
Why some turn bitter, why some go berserk.

CLEM and LYNDA TERRY sing:

Work experi-ness,
Work experi-ness,
Eight hours a day of unparalleled dreariness.
You'll take up gambling and vodka and beer-iness
When you experi-ness work.

LYNDA TERRY sings:

Outgoing oncologists,
Shy sociologists,
Clerks, ornithologists –
All do their chores,

Not always joyfully
But thinking employfully.
That's why, good-boyfully,
You must do yours.

TEACHERS sing:

Work experi-ness,
Work experi-ness,
Teachers delighted when pupils not here-iness.
Give us a treat of a week's disappear-iness.
Try to come back as not quite such a jerk.

TEACHERS, LYNDA and CLEM sing:

Work experi-ness,
Work experi-ness,
Round-robin, open-plan bad breath and leeriness.
At worst oppression, at best insincere-iness.
Go and experi-ness work.

LYNDA TERRY sings:

Engineers, metallurgical,
Chaplains, liturgical,
Ward sisters, surgical –
All know the score:
Work too hard, work a lot,
Work till your brain gets hot,
Do all the work you've got
Then find some more.

LYNDA and CLEM sing:

Work experi-ness,
Work experi-ness,
Rules that demand your fake-jolly adhere-iness,
No great vocation, no brilliant career-iness,
And you'll turn bitter, and you'll go berserk.

TEACHERS sing:

Work experi-ness,
Work experi-ness,
No Oscar Landrigan anywhere near-iness.
Think life's a joke? Well, you'll soon see it's seri-ness.
When you experi-ness work.

(As they're singing, OSCAR takes off his blazer, tie and shoes and arranges them somewhere nearby to look like a highly unconvincing Fake Oscar. Having done so, he sneaks offstage…)

LYNDA, CLEM and TEACHERS sing:

Go and experi-ness work!

LYNDA: Wait! (*She looks around.*) Where's he gone? Here's his uniform but he's not in it. (*To TEACHERS*) Today isn't a non-uniform day, is it?

MR M: No.

MISS N: In any case, his uniform is here.

LYNDA: Is it a non-children day, then, where the uniforms come in without the pupils who own them?

MISS W: (*tentatively, exchanging 'Is she mad?' looks with her colleagues*) We…er…we don't tend to have those at Pffisham School.

LYNDA: (*with grim satisfaction*) Well, there's another good idea I've had today, then. Uniforms that don't contain children would be much easier to control. Now, would somebody please find Oscar for me? I'm not leaving without him.

All TEACHERS and LYNDA hurry offstage. CLEM rolls her eyes and stays where she is.

SCENE 6

Outside Pffisham School, in the grounds of Idlewyld House. OSCAR is running away. He runs towards his family's gazebo, goes inside, closes the door and lowers the blinds. A few seconds later, we see BETHANY VOSS running up to the gazebo after him. She pulls open the door.

BETH: Caught you!

OSCAR comes back outside.

BETH: I can't believe you're actually running away from me. Talk about taking your rampant commitment-phobia to ever more absurd levels. It's *pathetic*.

OSCAR: (*confused*) What? I'm running away from *school*. They're trying to send me to a boring glue-making business to do work experience. (*He frowns*) What commitment-phobia, anyway? What does that even mean?

BETH: (*scornful*) Like you don't know! You refused to sign my prenuptial agreement.

OSCAR: (*slowly, as if he really fears she's mad*) Because we're not getting married, because we're *fifteen*. Also…that thing you called a pre-nup wasn't even a valid legal document. It was just some words you'd written down on a piece of paper, words which, if we were getting married, would actually leave you worse off if we ever split up. Let me try again to explain: I have a net worth of many millions, being the grandson of the late, great Harriet Landrigan. You have nineteen grand in an ISA.

BETH: Yes, and you're not getting your heartless hands on it.

OSCAR: I don't want it! My point is, if we *did* one day get married, it would be in your interests to lobby for the traditional approach, where everything we once owned individually belongs jointly to both of us, given–

BETH: And then when you wouldn't sign the document and I said I was going to two-time you instead of marrying you, and date Fred Croft behind your back, you shrugged and said 'Fine'.

OSCAR: (*sighs*) What was I supposed to say? It's up to you what you want to–

BETH: (*folds her arms*) Anyway, now Fred and I are engaged.

OSCAR: *What*? But we only had that conversation yesterday–

BETH: I have big goals, Oscar. So does Fred. He and I don't waste time, or hide from life. (*She looks the gazebo up and down, a sneery expression on her face.*)

OSCAR: Who is this Fred, anyway?

BETH: A neighbour. He doesn't go to Pffisham – he's home schooled. You know we've recently moved to Alpha Avenue?

OSCAR: Yeah. I came round to see you there once, at your new place. Your mum wouldn't let me in. It's a bit of a weird house, isn't it? Unfriendly looking. There are no windows in the side of the building that faces the road, just bricked up squares where windows used to be. The only proper window I could see was turned away from the street, facing the garden and almost completely covered up by an overgrown tree.

BETH: Ah, yes, but it's the address that counts, not the house itself. That's what Mum and Dad say. Alpha Avenue is the most expensive and exclusive street in town, and we're at number 2, which is *almost* number 1. And guess who lives at number 1? Fred Croft and his family! As Mum and Dad were saying last night, if Fred and I get married one day...well, then number 1 will practically belong to the Vosses, won't it? (*Sighs*) The Crofts' house is *beautiful*: tasteful grey brickwork, and the glossy red door looks positively regal!

OSCAR: (*baffled*) Okay. I mean...I don't really care about the front door colour of some dude I've never met, but... (*he shrugs*)

BETH: Fred writes me love letters. *He* has agreed to sign my pre-nup, and he's vowed never to touch the nineteen thousand pounds in my ISA. Unlike you, he's *thrilled* that I live so close to him.

OSCAR: What do you mean?

BETH: When I told you we'd moved house and said how happy I was to be so much nearer to you, because we'd be able to see each other absolutely all the time, you said...you said... (*She bursts into tears*)

OSCAR: I said, 'Maybe not all the time. Sometimes I'll have other things I need to do.' What's wrong with that?

BETH weeps more loudly.

OSCAR: Look, it sounds like you and Fred are pretty well-suited, so... good luck to you both.

BETH: (furious) Oh, so now you want me to see other boys, do you? You want an open relationship?

OSCAR: No! Not at all. Now I want a *closed* relationship, between you and Fred. Only. With me having nothing to do with either of you, but especially not with you – because, despite being hot, you're delusional. I mean, marriage? Fuck's sake!! I'm not ready to think about marriage. I'm a free and easy rolling stone who has gathered no moss. And I'm only fifteen.

BETH: Yes, and you always will be if you never commit to anything!

OSCAR: No. Next year I'll be sixteen.

BETH: Ugh, you're *impossible*… Moss-gathering is not bad, moss gathering is good. That's the whole point of that proverb!

OSCAR: No. It's the opposite.

BETH: Do me a favour, will you, Oscar? Just…*get lost!*

OSCAR: I *did* get lost. You came and found me. Stop finding me, if you don't like what you find.

BETH storms off. OSCAR goes back inside the gazebo and closes the door. BETH stops a few feet away, makes a loud, frustrated noise and pulls out her phone. She calls OSCAR, who answers from inside the gazebo.

OSCAR: Yo.

BETH: Go on, let's hear it.

OSCAR: Hear what? I thought the conversation was over.

BETH: (*sarcastic*) Oh, I'm sure you've plenty more to say! Please, tell me all about how things look from the wise perspective of a moss-free stone.

SONG NO. 5: SO LONG, GONE

BETHANY sings:

You're just not ready yet.
Do I expect you really
To bless the day we met,
Promise to love me dearly?
You think I'm hot and cool.
Also, I need to hear you
Because you've made a rule
Now I'll be living near you:
I should attach no strings,
We will not be exclusive.

OSCAR: Wait, you were the one who–

BETHANY sings:

I wanted different things.
You got sweary and abusive,
And now you're on the phone –

OSCAR: You called me!

You're bored one random Tuesday,
You're having a slow news day,
And I'm better than alone.

It's been a whole-year dance.
I've been the treasure squandered.
Now I'm your wasted chance.
How very far I've wandered,
And I've met someone new
Who treats me so much better –
Each look, each touch, each letter –
And I'm so very over you.

I've stripped you of the glow
Of my interpretations.
With all that I now know,
I'd ask for reparations,
But you just bore me blind
So there's no big procedure
To show you I don't need you.
Let's just say, 'Never mind'…

And if you're at my door
I'm sending you away.
Don't wanna save you for
A future rainy day,
And if you ask for more
You're gonna hear me say
That I'm long gone, I'm long gone.
I know what love means now.
It's not what you gave me.
There's no made or broken vow –
You needed to feel free,
So can you run with how
Nowhere-near-you I'll be
Now I'm long gone, I'm long gone?

OSCAR: (*to his phone*) You're not long gone, though – you're in my garden, wailing at me.

BETHANY sings:

I bless the day I met
Someone who loves me dearly
And saw what a pathetic
Loser you were really.
My mother labelled you
Profoundly unimpressive.
I thought that was excessive.
It could not have been more true,

And now you're on your own.
There's no one in your corner.
You're staring at your phone,
Wondering if you were born a
Fool or made that way
From all the stupid risks you've taken.
It'll feel like hell one day
And it's all of your own making.
You had a pot of gold
You thought would always be there
But now your heart's stone cold
Without my love or me there.
I'm your long-distant past.
There's no way to retrieve me,
To lose me or to leave me.
Watch me make this moment last

And if you're at my door
I'm sending you away.
Don't wanna save you for
A future rainy day
And if you ask for more
You're gonna hear me say
That I'm long gone, I'm long gone.

I know what love means now.
It's not what you gave me.
There's no made or broken vow.
You needed to feel free.
So can you run with how
Nowhere-near-you I'll be
Now I'm long gone, I'm long gone

(I'm… long… gone)

And if you ask for more
I'm sending you away,
Not gonna save you for
Some messed up rainy day
And if you beg for more
You're gonna hear me say
I'm so long gone, so long gone.
I know what love means now.
It's not what you gave me.
There's no made or broken vow.
Enjoy your being free.
Can you imagine how
Much joy there is for me
Now I'm long gone, I'm long gone?
So long gone, so long gone.
I'm long gone, I'm long gone.
I'm long gone, I'm long gone.
You're just not ready…yet!

GWEN LAPP appears, with three very tough, intimidating-looking adults dressed in Pffisham School uniforms. All three are wearing 'Prefect' badges and look grotesque. These are NATALIA, ISAAC and KATE.

GWEN L: Who is not ready yet? And for what?

BETH: (*putting her phone away*) N-nothing. No one. (*Her eyes keep drifting towards the gazebo and back again, nervously. She raises her voice.*) If you're looking for Oscar, he's not here, and… I haven't seen him anywhere near here.

GWEN: He's in that gazebo, isn't he? Since the two of you are no longer dating, there's no reason why you shouldn't tell me the truth.

BETH: (*angry*) Who told you we're not together any more? Did Oscar say that?

GWEN: I know everything that relates to Pffisham School and its pupils. (*Looking approvingly over her shoulder at the prefects*) My new prefects keep me very well informed.

BETH: (*defiant*) Well, you're wrong. If Oscar and I are no longer dating, that's only because…well, we got engaged this morning.

OSCAR, inside the gazebo, looks shocked and horrified.

BETH: So, now we're much more than dating. If you must know, Oscar has gone into London to buy me an engagement ring. (*Raises her voice and tilts her head in the direction of the gazebo*) From Hatton Garden in London. A diamond cluster.

OSCAR pushes open the door and makes a run for it. NATALIA, ISAAC and KATE run at him and restrain him.

NATALIA: (*in Russian accent*) I told you we find him, Meesees Lapp.

GWEN L: And I didn't doubt it. You're excellent prefects, all three of you. Now (*voice full of menace*) take him to TAGS where he shall do his work experience as planned.

OSCAR: These three goons aren't real prefects any more than Monsieur LeClay was a real French teacher. (*Emphatic, sore, as if he's determined to get Mrs Lapp to acknowledge this truth*) He was a clay model! At least these three are human, but they're obviously not children. They're all in their forties.

GWEN L: Don't be ridiculous.

OSCAR: I've heard the rumours. One of them's a former Russian intelligence agent, and another–

GWEN L: What claptrap! Enough! How dare you? I don't know who you think you are, but whoever it is, I promise you, you're not. You're a loathsome, disgraceful worm. And now you will stand there in silence, and listen to somebody else for a change. You will listen *to me…*

SONG NO. 6: FIND YOU

GWEN L sings:

You think you can win this war with school –
Treat all the staff like dirt, break each and every rule,
And to be fair to you, up to now that has proved true
But these new prefects are the best alive,
And when you skive,

They'll find you, find you,
Coming up behind you –
Fear them, obey them.
Guess how much we pay them,
Just to find you, find you,
Stifle, crush and grind you
Into detritus.
Don't even think about trying to fight us.

Natalia here, she joined us in Year 3,
From Guilden Morden primary, not the KGB.
Isaac came from The Perse…

OSCAR sings:

I've heard Mossad.

GWEN L gives him an 'Are you crazy?' look.

GWEN L sings:

Which is worse?
Kate's from a school called (covers her mouth with her hand to hide the name) *Broadmoor far away*
And every day they'll

Find you, find you,
Coming up behind you –
Dread them, avoid them.
No reprobate has yet destroyed them.

They'll find you, find you,
So let me remind you
You can't win here.
Soon it will be like you've never been here,

They'll find you,
They'll find you,
They'll find you....

The PREFECTS start to bundle Oscar into a car to take him to TAGS. He resists. BETH and GWEN LAPP stand watching.

BETH: (*distraught*) Oscar! Come back! (*When he continues to be dragged away, she raises her voice.*) Don't worry, everything will be fine. Work experience can't be that bad. Forget about my diamond cluster for now – that can wait!

SCENE 7

Pffisham School's Detention Unit. ASBO is still alone in there with the table, chair and green chicken on a tray. He's trying to find an escape route, scratching at the walls, punching doors, trying to break window locks and panes…

ASBO: Oscar! Oscar! When are you coming to break me out? I can't last much longer in here. (*Mutters to self, motivationally*) New iPhone, new iPhone…

The door unlocks.

ASBO: (*runs to the door*) Oscar?

The door opens. MISS NEARY and MISS WINDSOR enter. MISS NEARY is carrying a small bottle.

MISS N: Can you keep the noise down in here? I can't teach music with you screaming and wailing.

MISS W: Oscar Landrigan isn't coming to save you any time soon, I'm afraid.

ASBO: Why not?

MISS W: He's just left for his work experience placement. He won't be back in school for a week.

MISS N: We might be able to give you something else to look forward to, if you're interested.

MISS W: Assuming you're happy to cooperate. Because it's occurred to us that… (*Looks at MISS NEARY*)

MISS N: (*Clears her throat, stands up straighter*) A few pupils at Pffisham School have certain…conditions that require… well, medication. Now, you don't have any of those conditions, but what if what works for them might also work for you? What if we could turn you into a good boy via the wonders of modern pharmacology?

MISS W: (*alluringly*) The sort of boy who earns rewards.

ASBO: What rewards?

MISS N: Well, for instance, we could bring somebody in here for you to talk to. That's what happens, traditionally. Exemplary behaviour in the Detention Unit earns you the company of our very own Monsieur LeClay for the remainder of your…custodial sentence.

ASBO: He wouldn't be company. He's an inanimate object made of clay.

MISS N: (*whispers to MISS W*) I think Monsieur LeClay got thrown out after all the broadsheet hit pieces.

MISS W: Oh. I see. (*To ASBO)* Well, how about being allowed to leave this room, then? Early. Rejoin your friends?

ASBO: (*perks up*) Really?

MISS W: Really. Only if you cooperate, mind.

ASBO: With what?

SONG NO. 7: CAN WE DRUG YOU?

MISS N sings:

Can we drug you?

ASBO sings:

Can you… what?

MISS W sings:

Can we drug you?

ASBO sings:

Can you drug me? No, you can't.

MISS N sings:

Let me put it another way…

Can we drug you?
If you were a TV (and I'm so sad you're not),
We'd unplug you.
Certain minor adjustments would help quite a lot.
We could hug you –
With your sweet, harmless face, you're conceivably cute.
Hate to bug you
But we all need a week of immobile and mute.
Mogadon, Vicodin,
With some Night Nurse thrown in…
Can we drug, can we drug, can we drug you?

Let's sedate you!
It's in all of our interests, I'm sure you'll agree.
We don't hate you –
It's just sometimes you have way too much energy.
When we rate you
On this new 'Yuck! Boys!' scale, ranging one to fifteen,
We will fête you
As the most docile child Pffisham School's ever seen.
Give your mum a surprise
With your dim, blurry eyes.
Let's sedate, let's sedate, let's sedate you.

Can we drug you?
With a staff member's sign-off, it's all above board.
Please don't shrug. You
Know cool teenagers take drugs of their own accord?
As you glug, you
Feel your mind calming down, all stress melting away.
Hate to bug you
But this term has been tough. Let's improve it today.
With an 'Oh, what the heck!', chuck this muck down your neck.
Can we drug, can we drug, can we drug you?
Catatonia's a breeze. Just say, 'Thanks, Miss. Yes please.'
Can we drug, can we drug, can we drug you?

MISS W: Well? What do you think? (*She takes the bottle from MISS NEARY and waves it in front of ASBO's face.*) If you agree to take our special medicine, you can leave this room today. Right now, after your first dose.

ASBO: Absolutely not.

Both teachers look angry and frustrated. They rally.

MISS N: (*chirpily*) We'll be back in an hour or so to see if you've changed your mind.

MISS N and MISS W leave the room, locking the door behind them.

SCENE 8

Tribute Adhesive Gel Solutions (TAGS) offices. OSCAR sits in a chair, deep in thought, centre stage. CATHY, JEN, ANNIE, GRACE, LEO, MOLLY and PAUL crowd around him, watching him.

OSCAR: (*suddenly noticing them*) Er… can I help you?

ANNIE: What are you doing?

OSCAR: I'm thinking. Trying to solve a problem. Well, two problems, actually. A…really weird involuntary engagement situation, and a wrongfully imprisoned best friend.

LEO: But…aren't you going to set fire to anything?

OSCAR: No.

GRACE: How about spray-painting slanderous slogans and slurs all over the wall? Or maybe you could break that chair. (*She points.*)

OSCAR: Look, can you all leave me alone? Unless you've got any bright ideas about how to get my mate ASBO out of Pffisham School's Detention Unit while simultaneously persuading my…persuading this girl, Bethany, to– Ah, what's the point? (*He sighs.*)

CATHY: Maybe your friend ASBO wants to stay in the Detention Unit. It might be safe and cosy in there.

JEN: Yes, I've always thought it might be lovely to be confined to a prison – as long as one was treated kindly, of course. You know: properly looked after.

OSCAR: (*gives her a 'What the hell?' look*) No one wants to stay in the Detention Unit. That's why it's a punishment. (*He looks around at all of them.*) Can I ask you something? I've been forced to come here by my school and the county council, but…you lot are grown-ups. You have a choice. I know I've only been here for an hour, but this seems like the the most mind-numbingly boring office in the world.

LEO: It is! That's what we love about it. It's so stodgy and monotonous.

MOLLY: It's reliable!

PAUL: Predictable!

ANNIE: Unchanging! We know exactly what we'll be doing every day, for ever. It's perfect for neurotics like us.

JEN: What did your friend ASBO do, to get put in detention?

OSCAR: (*bitterly*) Nothing. Absolutely nothing. They wanted to make him suffer, so they banged him up on a baseless trumped-up charge.

LEO: Like poor Mr Surridge, our managing director.

OSCAR: What do you mean?

GRACE: Nothing.

LEO: We're not supposed to know. The story's too interesting and upsetting. It's all about injustice and heartbreak and suffering.

ANNIE: That's why Mr Surridge was so determined to take us all under his wing and create a humdrum environment for us here at TAGS. No one suffers in this building.

OSCAR: I do.

LEO: Not really. I mean, you can't possibly. There's no unfairness, no cruelty. Just wonderful boredom.

CATHY: Why did the school want to make ASBO suffer?

OSCAR: I don't think I should tell you. It's a crazy, messed-up story. If you hear it, you won't be bored any more.

ALL: Tell us, tell us! (*They all step back.*)

OSCAR: (*also stepping back*) Well, if you really want to know... Our school is supposed to be putting on a production of *Les Misérables.*

Enter PFFISHAM PUPILS including ASBO, MR MORRISON and MISS NEARY at front of stage. OSCAR and TAGS staff step back to make clear they're watching a flashback scene.

OSCAR: My mate ASBO got the main part: Jean Valjean. He's got a brilliant voice, so they overlooked the fact that he's a reprobate like me. And then one day, in the middle of a rehearsal, the police turned up...

MR M: (*to the pupils/cast members*) Come on, you lot! You can do better than that. Once more with feeling!

Enter INSPECTOR COODE and SERGEANT WILDERSPIN. The PUPILS, about to sing, stop with their mouths open, distracted. SERGEANT WILDERSPIN has his notebook and pen ready, and is also carrying a bound script.

INSP C: Good afternoon, all. I'm Inspector Coode. This is Sergeant Wilderspin.

MR M: Is something wrong? We're in the middle of rehearsing for the school musical. We're doing *Les Misérables*.

INSP C: Sergeant Wilderspin and I are here to discuss that very thing. We were on our way to a crime scene when we heard the song 'Castle on a Cloud' coming from one of your open windows. Evidently you are unaware of the new directive, which is unfortunate. Preventing crime is as important as solving it. Wouldn't you agree, Mr–?

MR M: Morrison. (*Smiles proudly*) Like Jim Morrison, lead singer of The Doors. (*Disappointed when this remark provokes no reaction*) Yes, I'm all in favour of preventing crime. Absolutely.

INSP C: Then why, might I ask, are you busy undermining our and the County Council's efforts by choosing *Les Misérables* as your school show?

MISS N: What on earth do you mean, Inspector?

INSP C: A musical that glorifies rebellious sentiment and revolutionary violence. (*He moves closer to MR M and says accusingly*) Guillotining all the posh people to death – there's no excuse for it!

MR M: But… Look, first of all that was a different French Revolution. *Les Mis* is about the–

INSP C: Is it really *so* important to you to encourage your pupils to chop off the heads of anyone more socio-economically fortunate than themselves? Well, you can't do it! Not any more. I won't have it, and neither will the county of Cambridgeshire. The new directive forbids, by law, the staging of any productions of *Les Misérables* in its original form in any school in the region, state-run or private.

MR M: (*flustered*) Well, I'm sorry, but…I've never heard of this new rule. It can't be enforceable, surely?

SERG W: (*to INSP C*) Mr Morrison doesn't think it's enforceable, sir.

INSP C: Well, he can find out the hard way if he likes. Or… (*smiles*) he can be sensible and switch over to the new, police-approved, health-and-safety-compliant version of the libretto, written by County Council environmental health officers. That's what all the other schools are doing.

SERGEANT WILDERSPIN waves the script in the air.

INSP. C: The title has been changed from *Les Misérables* to *Les Raisonnables*. That means 'The Reasonable Ones'. There's no violence in it, and no one is miserable. Initially, there are some characters who are a bit fed up, but they soon acquire a sense of perspective and agree to mediation sessions with the aristocrats, to arrive at a solution that's in everyone's best interests. There's a happy ending, naturally.

ASBO: (*stepping forward*) Excuse me, Inspector?

INSP. C: Yes, young man?

ASBO: That is *whack*, bruv. I mean…everything you've just said is absolutely insane.

INSP. C: Who is this insolent boy?

ASBO: My name's ASBO.

INSP. C: Of course it is.

ASBO: I'm playing Jean Valjean – but only if we can do the proper version of the show. Otherwise I'm out. And by the way, you can't just change a famous musical. The intellectual property belongs to…someone, presumably. You'd have to ask permission from whoever owns the rights, and they'd never say yes.

SERG W: Come now, young man. Give the new adaptation a chance.

ASBO: Absolutely no way. (*Jabs his finger at INSPECTOR COODE*) (*To rest of cast*) Man an *opp*, yo.

MISS N: Yes, why don't we give it a chance? I for one would love to stage *Les Raisonnables* – a non-violent, non-revolutionary musical. It sounds very civilised. Pass me the script, Sergeant Wilderspin. Jim, let's try singing one of the songs – maybe that will persuade the children that it's not so bad after all. Let's do this one: 'It Dawned on Me', the replacement for 'I Dreamed a Dream'. Look, here's the sheet music. (*She inspects it carefully.*) Wait… This isn't the same tune as 'I Dreamed a Dream'. The notes are completely different. I assumed the music would at least be the same.

INSP. C:	No. The council removed all chords, crotchets and quavers deemed likely to provoke revolutionary fervour.
GWEN L:	Oh. Well, I suppose that…might work? (*she sounds doubtful*) Let's give it a try.

MR MORRISON stands next to her. They get ready to sing.

SONG NO. 8: IT DAWNED ON ME

MISS N sings:

It dawned on me some time ago,
Posh people can't help being wealthy.

BOTH sing:

It's not too bad, the status quo
And envy really isn't healthy.

MISS N sings:

I am poor and life is tough,

MR M sings:

She is poor, her life is tough.

MISS N sings:

And I wish the rich would share things,

MR M sings:

And that pigs would fly as well,

MISS N sings:

But I can't just rob their stuff,

MR M sings:

You mustn't just rob their stuff.

MISS N sings:

Or chop off their heads at all.

MR M sings:

You can't. You can't! It's not okay!

Lights go down on INSP C, SERG W, MR MORRISON, MISS NEARY, ASBO and all rehearsal scene people, who exit as soon as OSCAR and TAGS STAFF step forward and OSCAR starts to speak…

OSCAR: Once ASBO saw that the show was going to be a bad joke and not the real deal, he refused to play Jean Valjean. And none of the rest of the cast could sing. Like, *at all.* So, the show's going to be a flop, and the teachers have had it in for ASBO ever since. That's why he's in detention. The story about him flipping his pencil case in the air and then throwing it at Mrs Lapp was a bare-faced lie.

CATHY: That's terrible. Poor ASBO. I wonder if we could somehow rescue him, using our adhesive gels.

JEN: How were you planning to set him free, Oscar?

OSCAR: It doesn't matter now. There's nothing I can do from here. And there's no way Waspy and 3-Strike can break him out without me there to mastermind the operation. (*Suddenly remembers*) What did you mean about Mr Surridge being locked up on a false charge?

CATHY: I'd like to know that too.

JEN: Me too. (*To OSCAR*) Cathy and I are new here. We only arrived today, like you. (*To LEO and the others*) Please tell us the story.

LEO: Well…you see, Mr Surridge had a son. His name was Luke…

They all huddle together. Lights go down.

SCENE 9

MR SURRIDGE's office at TAGS. The door is open. MR SURRIDGE is wearing pyjamas, dressing gown and slippers.

MR S: Diane! Duncan!

Enter DIANE and DUNCAN.

DIANE: Yes, Mr Surridge?

DUNCAN: Yes, Mr Surridge?

MR S: Can't you call me Derek? You are my brother and sister, after all.

DUNCAN: I believe it's important to maintain the proper hierarchical structures, Mr Surridge. If I allow myself to call you Derek, someone might hear me, and soon your entire staff will be referring to you as Degzie, or something equally disrespectful.

MR S: (*thoughtfully*). Degzie. Hmm. I don't think I'd mind being called Degzie.

DIANE: Well, we'd mind, even if you wouldn't.

MR S: Then I'll say no more about it. Now: where is this year's Terrible Boy? Wasn't he supposed to be arriving today?

DIANE: Yes, he's here. His name's Oscar Landrigan.

MR. S: Bring him in, then.

DIANE: In? You mean…in *here*? With you?

MR S: Well…no, maybe not. I don't want to get too close to him, or to anyone else. New people – they're not safe, you know.

DUNCAN: Well, quite!

DIANE: They're really not.

MR S: Put him in the room next door so that I can see him from a distance, and leave the door between the two rooms open.

DUNCAN: Very well, Mr Surridge.

DIANE and DUNCAN exit, then return a few seconds later with OSCAR and a chair. DUNCAN puts the chair down on the opposite side of the stage from MR SURRIDGE. He and DIANE stand back, between OSCAR and MR SURRIDGE, and prepare to relay their words to each other.

DIANE: Oscar, Mr Surridge would like to welcome you to Tribute Adhesive Gel Solutions.

MR SURRIDGE leans over, waves at OSCAR, then turns away and covers his face.

OSCAR: (*shocked*) Is that him? Is that Mr Surridge, the managing director?

DUNCAN: Yes. Why do you sound surprised?

OSCAR: His face. He looks exactly like The Generalist.

DIANE: The Generalist? Who's that?

Instrumental music of 'A Generalist Like Me' starts to play in the background.

OSCAR: John Danes. He's… This is going to sound weird, but he's my hero. I once helped him solve two murders. Unlike all my teachers at school, he likes me and believes in me. And unlike my parents, he doesn't think the fact that I'm incredibly rich means I shouldn't ever want or need to achieve anything.

DIANE: (*dubiously*) I see.

OSCAR: He does all sorts of strange jobs for all kinds of peculiar people – that's why he calls himself The Generalist. He's doing some work in New Zealand at the moment. I haven't seen him for ages, but whenever I'm in a tricky situation, I always ask him, in my head, what I ought to do. Even when he's not there to answer.

MR SURRIDGE, interest clearly piqued, stands up, walks over to the door and listens attentively.

OSCAR: The weird thing is, he always gives me great advice, even though it's not really him. It's just my imagination. Does that make sense?

DUNCAN: Not at all.

MR S: (*approaches, tentatively. Speaks passionately)* Yes. Yes, it does.

OSCAR: It's like, when ASBO got put in the Detention Unit. I asked John Danes, in my head, what was the best thing to do.

MR S: What did he say?

OSCAR: He said: 'Rewatch Season 1 of *Prison Break*. Then find the original architect's drawings of Pffisham School, memorise them, draw them, pretend it's your art project, find a gap in the building that you can tunnel into, and rescue your wrongly accused friend.' And then he said, 'I know you can do it, Oscar.'

MR SURRIDGE appears in the doorway, and finally OSCAR sees him again. They look at each other.

MR S: Hello, Oscar.

OSCAR: Yo, Mr Surridge.

MR S: I also ask my hero for advice sometimes, even though he's not there.

OSCAR: Who's your hero?

MR S: My son. Luke.

DIANE: Be careful, Mr Surridge. We don't want you getting all upset.

MR S: But, Diane, this is a most extraordinary coincidence! I remind Oscar of this John Danes chap, The Generalist, and he reminds me so much of… I mean, he doesn't look anything like Luke, but his manner, his energy…

SONG NO. 9: YOU REMIND ME OF SOMEONE

MR S sings:

Anyone who looks can see
A mysterious symmetry.
If you weren't you...

OSCAR sings:

If I weren't me...

BOTH sing:

I know exactly who you'd be...

OSCAR sings:

You remind me of someone who thought I was a star,
Who encouraged and praised me, and told me I'd go far,
Who said my life's adventure had only just begun...

MR S:

You remind me of someone I had to leave behind –
A lost-long-ago someone who's never left my mind,
An extraordinary someone who was my earth and sun.

MR S, DUNCAN and DIANE sing:

You remind me of someone.

MR S and OSCAR sing:

Anyone who looks can see,
I'm not him and he's not me,
You're not him and he's not you.
It makes no sense, and yet, it's true...

OSCAR sings:

You remind me of someone who told me I was bright,
An exceptional someone, who helped me get things right,
Who gave me endless chances in a world that gave me none...

MR S:

You remind me of someone I hoped that I could find,
Quite a rare sort of someone to cheer this daily grind,
Full of daft jokes and upheaval, as if work might be…fun?
You remind me of someone…

BOTH sing:

You remind me of someone
I never thought I'd meet,
A bizarre kind of someone, exactly up my street.
I don't yet know you very well, but when all is said and done
You remind me of someone,
You remind me of someone.

OSCAR: *(to MR SURRIDGE)* Is it true that you were wrongly accused of abducting and killing your son?

DIANE: Oscar, for pity's sake!

MR S: It's okay, Diane. Yes, it's true, Oscar.

OSCAR: That sucks. But you've given me an idea. Mr Surridge, I hope you don't mind me asking: how profitable is this company? It's just that…there doesn't seem to be much going on round here that's in any way dynamic or entrepreneurial.

MR S: (*with satisfaction*) Oh, TAGS is not at all profitable. We make a small loss every year. I don't mind. In fact, I rather like it. It feels…fitting. After I had to give up being a GP, my priorities changed. I didn't care about money any more.

OSCAR: That's foolish. You should definitely start caring about money again.

MR S: Ha! That's what my son Luke would say. You really are very like him, you know.

OSCAR: The thing is…I've already asked John Danes, in my head, what *he'd* do if he were managing director of TAGS and… well, his answer was quite interesting. He'd definitely make a few changes. I would too.

MR S: Would you, Oscar?

OSCAR: Yes. I would. Here's what I'd do…

There's a noise from offstage.

DIANE: Mr Surridge, there's someone coming. Quick, hide!

MR SURRIDGE hurries offstage.

OSCAR: Why does he have to hide? Isn't he meant to be here?

DUNCAN: He finds social interactions hard to cope with.

OSCAR: I reckon everyone here can cope with a lot more than they think they can. Hasn't anyone ever told you that it's only by going outside your comfort zone that you can evolve to your highest potential and become a brilliant example of what's possible?

DUNCAN: No. That sounds like dangerous propaganda.

OSCAR: I had a detention every single day after school last term. It was tough, but I survived.

DIANE: What did you do to get all those detentions? I'm sure you deserved them.

OSCAR: I didn't, actually. My only crime was to keep pointing out that the new French teacher was a clay model and not a real person. No one believed me, until I proved it by slicing off his arm. His *clay* arm.

DIANE: (*brightly, to audience*) He could have stuck it back on with one of our adhesive gels!

OSCAR: Guys, listen… Don't get too attached to this whole…glue thing you've got going on here.

DIANE: What do you mean? We're very attached to our glue!

OSCAR: That's a pity…because…(*thoughtfully, working it out as he speaks*) I think I might be about to make some changes around here. Some *big* changes…

Lights go down…

End of ACT ONE

ACT TWO

SCENE 1

Pffisham School hall, rehearsals for Les Raisonnables *are underway, and on stage are MR MORRISON, MISS NEARY and Pffisham School pupils, including BARTIE VOSS, the school's star pupil. BARTIE stands next to MR MORRISON, as if he's one of the teachers, holding and reading a copy of the* Les Raisonnables *libretto.*

MR M: Now, cast, listen to the way I sing the first two lines, and then sing them after me. Miss Neary will accompany you on the piano. All right?

PUPILS: (*mumbling*) Yes, sir.

MR M: It's all very well to say 'Yes, sir', but last time we tried it, nobody opened their mouth and my solo effort was followed by complete silence. So, let's have some actual singing this time, please. Right, here goes…

MR M sings: *This is how things look to me. Tell me, how do they–*

BARTIE: Excuse me, sir?

MR M: Bartie, for pity's sake–

BARTIE: I've just worked it out.

MR M: What? It had better be important. You might be our star pupil and our new Jean Valjean, but that doesn't mean you can interrupt whenever you feel like it.

BARTIE: It's the lyrics, sir. Didn't you say this song's the replacement for 'The Song of Angry Men'?

MR M: If you mean 'Do You Hear the People Sing?', then yes. This…substitute song is called 'I'm Sure We Can All Agree'. (*He sighs*) As I've already explained, Jean Valjean doesn't sing it. He sings other songs. You can't hog the limelight all the time, Bartie.

BARTIE: (*looks hurt*) That's not my intention at all, sir. I merely wish to point out that the lyrics to this new song can be sung to the exact tune of the old song – to the music of 'Do You Hear The People Sing?' Put these words and that tune together and it works perfectly. (*Sounds satisfied, like he's solved a difficult puzzle.*) How very clever of whoever it was at the County Council that wrecked the original musical.

MISS N: 'Wrecked'? Bartie, if you're going to undermine morale, I'm sure we can find someone else to play the role of–

BARTIE: Did I say 'wrecked'? I meant 're-interpreted'. 'Adapted'. (*Turns back to the script, flicking pages, leaning in to see more clearly*) And look, the same's true of 'It Dawned on Me'. Those lyrics precisely fit the rhythm and tune of 'I Dreamed a Dream.'

MR M: (*half impatient, half admiring*) How on *earth* did you work that out?

BARTIE: There's a reason why I'm the school's star pupil, sir.

MR M: Yes, well. Very impressive, as always, Bartie. But now I really must get on with teaching your fellow cast members to forget the good song and learn the rubbish one, I'm afraid.

MISS N: (*Shocked*) Mr Morrison! If you're going to be a nay-sayer who undermines morale, I'm sure I can find someone else to help me– (*breaks off, frowns, shakes head*). Actually, I don't think I could.

MR M: (*vehemently*) I *know* you couldn't. You're stuck with Muggins here, who was stupid enough to volunteer. And I'm stuck with this lot (*points to the droopy cluster of children who failed to sing*), and we're all stuck with this stupid, politically correct– (*He breaks off*) Ach, forget it. I give up. (*Plastering fake smile on his face.*) Right, cast, can I please have your full attention? Sing along with me, please, as loud as you can.

SONG NO. 10: I'M SURE WE CAN ALL AGREE

MR M sings: *This is how things look to me.*
Tell me, how do they look to you.
We can arrive at a consensus if we hear both points of view.
If we focus on shared goals
Here in this room for fourteen days,
All of our lives might then improve in a range of ways.

MISS N sings:

With a positive approach, we can proceed efficiently.
We will start with Item A, and then move on to Item B.
There's plenty of biscuits and coffee and peppermint tea…

ALL sing as they exit the stage:

> *This is how things look to me.*
> *Tell me, how do they look to you?*
> *We can arrive at a consensus if we hear both points of view.*
> *If we focus on shared goals*
> *Here in this room for fourteen days,*
> *All of our lives might then improve in a range of ways…*

Lights go down on them singing.

SCENE 2

TAGS offices. Split scene. OSCAR on one side of the stage, MR SURRIDGE on the other. There's an open door between them, and MR SURRIDGE is in his office, typing on a laptop, dressed in different pyjamas, dressing gown and slippers. OSCAR has his phone in his hand. MR SURRIDGE is typing a message to OSCAR. The Overture is playing in the background, quietly, on a loop.

MR S (VOICEOVER):

Dear Oscar, you asked me about my son earlier today. I gave you the briefest of responses: yes, I was suspected of abducting and killing Luke. I'd have liked to give you a fuller answer, but as a confirmed recluse, I don't have conversations any more, and certainly not ones that contain an excess of detail. Therefore, I hope you will forgive me for sending you this email, which contains the entire story.

OSCAR: Ah, *what*?! I have to read a whole story email? Long, bruv.

MR S (VOICEOVER):

My son Luke has always been something of a free spirit. Hard to contain. School never suited him, and he often got into trouble. One day, he took it too far. He produced a ping pong ball in the middle of a Chemistry exam, and started to bounce it on the desk, distracting his fellow pupils. The whole class failed the exam. I was summoned to the school and told that Luke was to be placed in the Detention Unit for a month. I was devastated, naturally. I knew what that meant, that it wasn't much different from being in prison. I arrived home from my meeting with the head teacher feeling quite desolate. I wanted to complain, but my then wife, Eve – Luke's mother.... Well, she was very much the boss in our marriage, and she insisted that Luke's school was an excellent establishment. If they judged such a harsh punishment to be necessary, she said, then it must be. But the trouble is, Oscar...it *wasn't* an excellent school. I was always too afraid of Eve to tell her that. Oh, the buildings were nice enough, I suppose, and one paid through the nose to send one's child there, but I always thought it was a dreadful institution nevertheless, run by power-crazed nutcases. And, though Eve could never see it, the warning signs were there from the start. The year Luke joined, the position of Head Boy was awarded to a dog. Yes, you read that right, Oscar. The bossiest parents didn't yet have a child old enough to shoulder such a daunting responsibility, so they nominated the family pet. Astonishingly, the head agreed to this arrangement.

OSCAR: (*mutters*) Sounds like my school. Wait...(*frowns*) There can't be two schools that...

MR S: I'm not sure I should tell you this, Oscar, but...I'm afraid you're all too familiar with the hellhole I'm describing. I'm talking about Pffisham School. That's where my son was a pupil.

OSCAR: OMG. I knew it! That's Horatio Voss he's talking about, Bethany and Bartie's dog. That's right, Horatio *was* Head Boy for a while. The Vosses didn't have any kids of the right age, and they convinced the school that their Bedlington Terrier would do the job better than anyone else's child.

MR S (VOICEOVER):

I hadn't been home long, after my meeting with the then headmaster, Mr Friend, when I received a phone call to say Luke had gone missing from the Detention Unit. Next thing I knew, the police were arresting me. Soon after that I was charged with the abduction and murder of my own son. Ridiculous! Apparently a witness said I was close to the school at around the time Luke was locked away – well, of course I was there! The head had summoned me, for the meeting I've just told you about. That doesn't make me a kidnapper or a murderer. The very idea that I could harm my own beloved child…

OSCAR: I'm going to have to look this case up. (*Typing on his phone*) Luke…Surridge…disappearance…

MR S (VOICEOVER):

According to Pffisham School, Luke was taken to the Detention Unit by a revolting sadist who was once a French teacher at Pffisham and is now the head: Gwen Lapp. She locked him in there, and when she next went to check on him, he had vanished. I don't know how anyone ever imagined that I might have been able to get hold of the keys to the unit to get him out, but there we are. There was never any solid evidence against me, just people talking nonsense. Eventually, after a long stretch behind bars, all charges against me were dropped. By then, I'd lost my wife and my GP practice as well. All my money had gone on lawyers' fees. I had to start again with nothing. Only my brother and sister stood by me, Diane and Duncan. Together, the three of us started Tribute Adhesive Gel Solutions. We wanted it to be more than a business. The most important thing to us was that TAGS should be a safe haven for people who, for whatever reason, can't take any more and want to hide here with us forever in a comforting state of hibernation.

OSCAR: (*thoughtfully, reading from his phone*) Wait, what's this? Karen Beaton, host of the 'Justice For Locked Room Luke' podcast, was originally a witness…blah blah blah…. positive that she saw Derek Surridge driving away from the school that day with his son Luke in the passenger seat. Both of them, she claims, were wearing…(*He looks up, as if something has struck home*)…pyjamas. (*Looks over at MR SURRIDGE, then back at his phone, continues to read aloud*) Derek Surridge strenuously denies this, but Karen Beaton told police, 'I know what I saw.'

MR S (VOICEOVER):

Oscar, one of the reasons I wanted to write to you and tell you all of this is that…well, you're only here for a week. That means you'll soon be gone. I don't know why, but I find that thought alarming. You're the boy I've been looking for, you see. Ever since, Luke disappeared, I… Well, I had this idea to make it an annual thing: bring Pffisham's most Terrible Boy of the year to TAGS for a week of work experience, in the hope I might find someone like my son to….I don't know. Fill the void, I suppose. Luke was the school's original Terrible Boy, you see. That's what all the teachers used to tell me and write in his reports: that he was nothing but a menace. But he wasn't. He was the best person I've ever known. And…you're so similar to him, Oscar. The other Terrible Boys who have come here have been no more than louts and vandals, but you… You're full of gusto and initiative, though you try to hide it. I'm hoping you might be able to help me find...well, to solve... I mean, ahem, I'm perhaps not making myself clear...

OSCAR: What?! How am I supposed to find a boy who's been missing for years?

MR S (VOICEOVER):

I hope you won't think me presumptuous in saying this, but...Luke is alive. I know it, in my heart. I would know if anything awful had happened to him. He's alive, Oscar – which means he can be found, and something tells me that you might be just the person to find him. Yours sincerely, your temporary boss, Derek Surridge.

OSCAR: (*typing on his phone*) Dear Mr Surridge, I'm afraid I don't know where your son Luke is, so I can't help you with that. I just tried asking my hero, John Danes, in my head but he hasn't answered me yet, so I'm pretty sure he doesn't know either. However, I can help you with *something*: making your business more profitable and... well, just generally better. Can we have a meeting almost immediately to discuss my amazing plans? Yours sincerely, your temporary Terrible Boy, Oscar Landrigan.

Exit OSCAR.

MR S: (*terrified and angry*) Diane! Duncan!

Enter DIANE and DUNCAN.

DIANE: What is it, Mr Surridge?

MR S: He wants a meeting! Do you think that means I'll need to put on proper clothes?

DIANE: Of course not, Mr Surridge.

DUNCAN: Who wants to meet you?

MR S: Oscar Landridgan. I wrote to him… Oh, dear. I suppose if you start a conversation with somebody…

DUNCAN: No good can come of a conversation with a Terrible Boy, Mr Surridge.

MR S: He wants to make some changes, here at TAGS.

DUNCAN: What? How dare he intrude upon our soothing stagnation with his irresponsible talk of change!

MR S: I'll see him. I want to hear what he has to say.

DIANE: Mr Surridge, with all due respect….

MR S: Arrange the meeting, please, Diane. Duncan (*solemn pause*) – find me a new, smart pair of pyjamas.

SCENE 3

TAGS office. JEN, CATHY and TAGS STAFF are all sitting cross-legged on the floor, being addressed by OSCAR.

OSCAR: All right, listen. We've got important work to do today, and none of it has anything to do with glue, apart from… well, if we all *stick* together in our determination to succeed, we'll achieve great things. Who's in?

ANNIE: I've heard enough. Count me out. I want to strive to achieve ordinary things, not great ones. That way I know already, even before I've tried, that I won't fail.

All the TAGS employees nod their agreement with ANNIE.

OSCAR: Look, I knew none of you would be keen. In the short time I've been here, I've come to understand how you all think, and actually…(*he grins*) it's inspired me.

GRACE: (*looks pleased*) Really?

OSCAR: Yep. The lack of ambition here is so unbearably stultifying, it's made me come over all innovative and entrepreneurial.

JEN: Oh, dear. I hope that isn't contagious.

OSCAR: Here's what we're going to do. Trigger warning: it involves leaving the building.

TAGS STAFF all shriek and gasp.

OSCAR: And that's the last trigger warning you're getting. By the end of the week – no, by the end of the *day* – I'm going to turn you into people who aren't scared of any words, phrases, sentences, ideas, thoughts or opinions.

CATHY: But…you're talking about (*lowers voice*) change. Change is the thing that terrifies us most of all.

OSCAR: (*Sighs*) Okay, clearly a motivational anecdote is needed… but which one? (*Brightens*) I know: I'll tell you about the time I was very nearly expelled but, incredibly, managed to talk my way out of it – or rather, to *sing* my way out of it. It was only a couple of weeks ago, so I remember it well.

Enter ASBO, 3-STRIKE and WASPY, smoking cigarettes and holding bottles of wine and cans of lager. They go and form a huddle on one side of the stage, around a standing ashtray/bin of the kind you see on pavements outside pubs and hotels.

OSCAR: Me and my mates were hanging out in the woods on the other side of my family's gazebo, in the grounds of our house, smoking rollies, bakin' off, heavy chillin', you know? (*TAGS staff look mystified*) We were minding our own business, when suddenly we saw the enemy advancing: Miss Neary, our music teacher, looking furious. She'd got my mum and dad with her too.

Enter MISS NEARY, PETER LANDRIGAN and CLEMENCY LANDRIGAN.

PETER: What's going on here, Oscar? And what on earth is that monstrosity disfiguring my woodland? (*He points at the stand-up ashtray.*)

OSCAR: Who, Ash? He's our ashtray that doubles as a bin, and he's better at multi-tasking than any teacher at Pffisham School. (*To MISS N*) If you need another non-human teacher at any point, now that Monsieur LeClay's been cancelled, I'd say Ash is your ideal candidate. (*To PETER*) He keeps our woods nice and tidy.

MISS N: You see, Mr Landrigan? This is the sort of insolence that Oscar –

PETER: (*wearily*) Yes, I know, I know. Oscar, for pity's sake! Apologise to Miss Neary and then return to your music lesson. And the rest of you. Apparently you all escaped via an open window.

MISS N: I didn't realise at first. I mistook the clanking of their plastic bags full of acolholic beverages for…well, for percussion instruments.

PETER: Oscar, I'm afraid I simply won't tolerate–

CLEM: Oh, don't be a bore, Peter. You haven't heard Oscar's side of the story yet. (*Smiles sweetly at OSCAR*) I'm sure there's a perfectly reasonable explanation, isn't there, darling boy?

OSCAR: Correct as ever, dearest mother. Indeed there is: an amazing explanation. I don't suppose you…(*hopefully, to CLEM*) might have any thoughts as to what it might be? No? Right, well, in that case, give me a minute to… assemble it…

PETER: A reasonable explanation? Clemency, it's the middle of the perishing school day and our son has a beer in one hand and a cigarette in the other!

MISS N: I'm afraid we're well past the last warning stage, Mr Landrigan. Mrs Lapp is talking about expelling him. Bringing alcohol into school, truanting whenever he feels like it–

OSCAR: Nooooo, that's not what's happened here at all. Truanting? Far from it. This is a huge misunderstanding. The truth is, Miss Neary, that your lesson about… (*Turns to his friends, whispers*) Anyone remember what it was about?

3-STRIKE: The history and traditions of English folk music. Big yawn.

WASPY: (*under breath*) Yeah, like…don't bore me now. Bore me later.

ASBO: (*under breath*) Try not to bore me while you're trying to bore me.

OSCAR: Miss, the way you were…holding forth about English folk music, it… (*he puts his hand on his heart*) well, it ignited something deep within us. Suddenly, all we wanted to do was write a folk song of our own, so we came here to the woods for inspiration. (*Nods happily, pleased with his lie.*)

PETER: What rubbish! Miss Neary, I apologise for my son's abject dishonesty.

OSCAR: (*earnest, charming*) No word of a lie, Miss.

MISS N: I'm afraid I don't believe you, Oscar.

OSCAR: That's understandable. I'm not always scrupulously honest in my dealings with Pffisham School. But this is quite different. I'm thoroughly reliable at the moment.

MISS N: I see. So you've written a folk song, then, have you?

OSCAR: (*briefly fazed, then rallies*) Um…yes, yes we have! Quite splendid it is too. Would you like us to sing it to you?

ASBO: (*hisses*) Oscar, what the…? What if she says yes? Like, think ahead, man!

OSCAR: (*to MISS N*) And then we can forget all this nonsense about you expelling me. Once you've heard our song, you'll be wanting to award us this year's music prize, not get rid of us.

MISS N: Let's hear it, then. (*Folds arms*)

OSCAR clears his throat and steps forward.

SONG NO. 11: DEAR STAND-UP ASHTRAY

OSCAR sings : to the tune of traditional folk song 'The Ash Grove'

Beyond the gazebo
Where birds chirp their greeting,
The reprobates' meeting
Takes place in this glade.
When parents are absent
And homework is distant,
Our boozing remains consistent,
Our hearts unafraid.

'Tis here, where teenagers
Stand secretly smoking,
Prank-calling and joking
The whole livelong day,

That joy flows unbounded,
And great plans are seeded,
And that's why we needed
The stand-up ashtray.

Turns to PETER…

For every landowner
Who cares for his acres,
Protects from mess-makers
The ancestral yard,
So call him delinquent
And tell him he's grounded.
The ashtray he found did
Keep grass blades unscarred.

WASPY sings:

Oh ashtray-cum-dustbin
Not found so much as stolen,
Our young hearts are swollen
With deep gratitude.
So stalwart, so sturdy
It stands here and catches
Our cig ends and our spent matches
And remnants of food.

ASBO sings:

When GCSEs threaten
To rain down on us new traumas,
You're here for us non-conformers
You stick by our side,

OSCAR sings:

Rectangular and faithful,
So much more than a container,
This hard-core hard-work-disdainer
Avows you with pride.

All REPROBATES sing:

'Tis here where teenagers
Stand furtively smoking,
Tik-Tok-ing and joking
The whole livelong day,

OSCAR sings:

And you do not judge us,
Or say 'No, I will not let you.'
We love you. We'll ne'er forget you,
Dear stand-up ashtray.

CLEM: Oh, darling, that's simply spectacular! Isn't it Peter? What a talented boy you are!

PETER looks unconvinced. MISS NEARY is too astonished to speak.

Exit PETER, CLEM, MISS NEARY, ASBO, 3-STRIKE, WASPY. Stage goes back to OSCAR and TAGS staff scene.

OSCAR: My brilliant plan worked. I didn't get expelled, and me and my mates almost won the music award, until Mrs Lapp said we weren't allowed to win because our folk song glamorised the immoral and occasionally lethal pursuits of stealing, drinking alcohol and smoking. (*Leans in, starts to sound zealous and preachy*) The point is, I had no idea, when I offered to sing that song to Miss Neary, if I'd be able to make one up off the top of my head like that while drunk. For all I knew, it could have been a dismal failure. But it wasn't – because I deliberately dared myself. I stretched myself and, in doing so, proved that I was capable of so much more than I'd ever have thought possible. My brilliant brain came up with the goods, and the skills and the self-belief. So did ASBO's. So did Waspy's. See what I'm saying? Attempt the impossible, and often you end up proving to yourself that it's not so impossible after all.

CATHY: Well, that's all very well for you, Oscar, but we're not like you. We're timid and inept. We're always frightened, of everything.

OSCAR: (*frustrated*) You need to stop telling yourselves that about yourselves, as if it's an intrinsic part of who you are. Say instead: 'Bring it on, whatever it might be. I fear nothing!'

PAUL: Are you quite *mad*? (*Turns to MOLLY*) Is he mad?

OSCAR: (*sighs*) All right, if an inspiring mission isn't your bag, I'll make it easy for you. All you need to do is listen and obey.

MOLLY: (*relieved*) Oh, we're good at doing that.

OSCAR: Okay, great. Leo, Molly and Grace – you're going to track down Karen Beaton, host of the 'Justice for Locked Room Luke' podcast, and ask her some questions. I'll give you a list. Paul, Jen Annie and Cathy – you're going to go to Pffisham School and carry out some investigations there. (*A secretive, knowing look appears on his face.*) And maybe do something else while you're there too, something involving adhesive gels…

PAUL: Oh, yes, please – we'd love to take lots of glue with us!

MOLLY: We adore glue.

OSCAR: (*stands tall, looks out to audience*) Good, because, do you know what I love? Being implausibly impressive and blowing my own mind. Maybe, with your help, I can save TAGS, break ASBO out of the Detention Unit and find Luke Surridge, all at the same time!

SCENE 4

BARTIE and BETHANY VOSS pass each other on the corridor at Pffisham School.

BETH: Bartie, wait! Come back. I need your help.

BARTIE: Is this about Oscar Landrigan? Dumped him, did you, in favour of Fred Croft?

BETH: Yes, but things have moved on since then. Oscar and I are engaged.

BARTIE: (*frowns*) You jest?

BETH: No, we really are betrothed to one another, in a definitely going to get married and he's buying me a diamond cluster kind of way. So don't say anything mean about him.

BARTIE: Oh, I don't mind young Landrigan. I'm rather fond of him, actually. He's clever. Like me, he approaches every challenge in the manner of one who expects to be victorious. Shortly before he went off to do his work experience, he and I had a brief discussion about the abhorrent vandalism that poor *Les Misérables* has suffered at the hands of the County Council's health and safety officers. ASBO was quite right to resign from the role of Jean Valjean. I was considering doing the same, until Oscar set me straight.

BETH: How? What did he say?

BARTIE: He reminded me that boycotting Pffisham's big show would clash with my star pupil brand, and he was dead right. He had a better idea. Somehow he knew – from his mother, I think – that the person who might have rather a lot to say about the aforementioned vandalism is a chap called Cameron Mackintosh. He's some sort of musical theatre magnate. Oscar seemed to think he would put his considerable resources behind saving the real *Les Mis*. You know: take on the council twerps, Cambridgeshire Police *and* Pffisham School. In Oscar's view, if that particular fight were to play out, Mr Mackintosh would win – and if he did, then I'd be able to play the lead role in a brilliant musical instead of a ridiculous one.

BETH: Oh, my brilliant, talented Oscar! There's no problem he can't solve.

BARTIE: Well, it's not quite as simple as that, I'm afraid. Naturally, I followed up what sounded like an excellent suggestion, and managed to secure an in-person interview with Mr Mackintosh. I was quite horrified to find him already aware of the entire dismal situation. Worse still, he said he doubted he could do anything to remedy it. He told me he'd tried, but after some nasty, threatening emails from a Sergeant Wilderspin, he gave up. 'Ah well,' he said, in a tone of utmost resignation. 'I suppose it was magical while it lasted. There's nothing more that can be done now.'

BETH: Oh, no. That's so sad. So what did you do?

BARTIE: I told him he needed to buck up and stop being so defeatist. That didn't go down well. We got into a bit of a row, actually, which wasn't helping anything, so I excused myself, went outside and messaged Oscar to ask for advice.

BETH: And? I bet he saved the day, didn't he?

BARTIE: As a matter of fact, he sort of did. He told me to go straight back to Mackintosh's office and make my best possible case, but in the form of a song with a catchy tune. Told me he'd done something similar to avoid getting expelled recently. So I did. Back to the office I went, and made straight for the piano in the corner of the room. Gently elbowed a chap called Andrew Something-or-other out of the way – he must have gone in there while I was texting Oscar–

BETH: (*gasps*) Not Andrew Lloyd Weber?

BARTIE: Yes, that's the one. I moved him aside and began to play the music I was composing on the spot in my effortlessly brilliant mind, while making, lyrically, an irrefutable argument for never giving up…

BARTIE walks to the front of the stage and mimics playing a piano…

SONG NO. 12: SOMETHING CAN BE DONE

BARTIE sings:

Something can be done.
Something can always be done.
It's too soon to say,
'Let's quit now, we've not had a bad run.'
Be a little braver, be a little stronger.
Make that good run last a little longer, longer.

Bad things can be changed.
Wrong things can sometimes be changed.
There's no need to stay
Out of sorts, dispossessed or estranged.
Though it's not straightforward,
Though it might be scary
Let's keep Les Mis *revolutionary, very.*

Something can be done.
We have problems and then there are none.
It was bad enough with the songs cut
For BBC1.
Charmingly persuasive,
Never with coercion,
Let's keep asking
For the better, proper version.

There's no need for blame
Though, politely, the point might be made:
You can't change the name,
Or the tunes or the words, I'm afraid.
Why dismember this show
When to write a whole new one
Is a thing that can always be done?
Battles may be lost. More often they are won
When we say
Something can always be done.
Something can always be da-da-da-da-da-da-da-da-da,
Done!

BETH: Bartie, that's superb! I bet Cameron Mackintosh changed his mind and approach completely once he heard that.

BARTIE: Indeed he did. He and his friend Andrew were singing along and clapping by the time I go to the last verse – and full to the brim with the sort of fighting spirit that makes miracles happen. So… now we wait. Can their newly-installed optimism defeat the police and the County Council? That's the big question.

BETH: Oh, of course they can. I believe in them – and in you, Bartie. That's why I want your help. I can't do this on my own.

BARTIE: Do what?

BETH: First, end my relationship with Fred Croft somehow. Tell him something encouraging and tactful so that he isn't too sad. And then…the harder task…persuade Mum and Dad to be happy about me getting engaged to Oscar.

BARTIE: Hmm. That will be a challenge. Still….

BARTIE sings quietly as he strolls off stage:

> *Something can always be…da da da da da da da da da. Done!*

SCENE 5

TAGS offices. MR SURRIDGE is sitting in a chair, wearing his new smart pyjamas. OSCAR knocks at the door. MR SURRIDGE first leaps up and hides behind his chair. Then he remembers he has asked for this meeting, so he goes back and sits down in the chair.

MR S: Come in.

Enter OSCAR.

OSCAR: Morning, Mr Surridge. Nice weather today, isn't it?

MR S: I don't know. I never look out of windows if I can help it.

OSCAR: Well, take it from me: it *is* a nice day – the perfect day to change your entire business model.

MR S: I don't change things, Oscar. Ever.

OSCAR: *You* don't have to change anything.

MR S: Good.

OSCAR: I've done it for you. I've already implemented a sweeping programme of transformation.

MR S: What? But…

OSCAR: TAGS is reborn! All the old staff are gone.

MR S: Gone?

OSCAR: Yes. I've, er…put them to work elsewhere.

MR S: But…then who will sell our adhesive gels?

OSCAR: No one. From now on, TAGS won't be selling any adhesive gels. Mr Surridge, do you remember you told me that you sometimes ask your hero, your son Luke, for advice? In your head? And then it feels as if he answers you? And I told you that I do the same with my hero John Danes, The Generalist?

MR S: Ye-es.

OSCAR: Well, that got me thinking: if you and I both do it, other people must do it too. And more still might want to who don't do it already.

MR S: I suppose so.

OSCAR: (*triumphantly*) That's our new business model. Instead of selling boring glue, we're going to be an advice-giving service. And our USP is this: customers will come in, tell us who their heroes are, and our staff will pretend to *be* their heroes, while giving them advice. Think of the money we'll make! Who *wouldn't* pay over the odds to get advice from someone pretending to be their hero, the person they most admire in the world? And even if someone's got a hero who's dead, like Winston Churchill or Marilyn Monroe, that's no barrier. One or more of our new recruits can easily pretend to be both! (*Walks to the front of the stage and talks directly to the audience.*) It was the name 'Tribute' in 'Tribute Adhesive Gel Solutions' that gave me the idea. A tribute band is a band that mimics another, more famous band. We're going to mimic people's heroes!

MR S: Oscar, this will never work. I don't want to do it. I mean, if there was *some* element of adhesive gels involved, I might feel differently, but…(*he turns to face OSCAR.*) Also, *what* new recruits? Where would we get them from? According to you, TAGS currently has no staff. And what about the name: TAGS. The 'AG' bit in the middle stands for 'adhesive gels'. Please don't tell me you've changed the name?

OSCAR: No, we're still going to be TAGS. Only now it stands for Tribute Advice-Giving Service. And we *have* got staff. I've hired a truly stellar team. Mr Surridge, allow me to introduce you to your new employees!

Enter the WRONGLY ACCUSED: GEORGE, DANNY, SERENA, HENRY and WENDY. They walk in and stand in a line at the front of the stage, facing the audience. Their body language is hostile and defensive. They do not look promising.

GEORGE: If you don't want us here, Mr Surridge, just say so and we'll leave. You never have to see any of us again if you'd rather not.

DANNY: We're used to feeling unwelcome and used to being sent away.

SERENA: We've come to expect it.

HENRY: We've given up all hope of fair treatment.

GEORGE: Really, nothing you say can affect us. We've heard it all before. So if you're going to send us packing, do us a favour and do it now.

SERENA: Yes, get it over with.

DANNY: We've made a bet with Oscar. He says you'll ask us to stay, but no one has done that for many years.

HENRY: None of us can believe it's going to happen now.

GEORGE: You might not understand this, Mr Surridge, but the certainty that one will be rejected can be almost comforting.

DANNY: The opposite is also true: the possibility of acceptance can be rather alarming.

MR S: (*pointing at WENDY but speaking to OSCAR*) Why doesn't that one speak?

GEORGE: She used to. She gave up using words two years ago, in protest. To show how disgusted she is by the world and everyone in it.

WENDY nods vigorously. MR SURRIDGE takes OSCAR to one side.

MR S: Oscar, I'm sure there's a reason why you've chosen these people, but...I'm concerned. They don't seem to have much of a 'Can Do' attitude. Impersonating people's heroes in order to give them advice is a risky and delicate venture – one that could easily fail. What makes you think these characters are right for the job? One of them appears to have taken a vow of silence.

OSCAR: She'll start speaking soon enough, once you've promised to give her a chance. They'll all cheer up once you've told them you want them here.

MR S: But I *don't* want them here.

DANNY: (*to the other WRONGLY ACCUSED*) See? It's the same wherever we go. Come on, let's not waste any more of our time. (*He turns to leave.*)

OSCAR: Wait! It's nothing personal. Mr Surridge doesn't know who you are. All he means is that he wants his old staff back. He wants to sell adhesive gels, not advice from pretend heroes. At the moment he has a fixed mindset, but we're going to show him why it's always better to have a growth mindset.

GEORGE: There's no point having a growth mindset when all the minds around you are fixed.

DANNY: If Mr Surridge doesn't know who we are, don't you think you ought to tell him?

HENRY: He's supposed to be one of us. I can't believe he really is.

OSCAR: He is. Wait. Leave it to me. (*Turns to* MR SURRIDGE) Mr Surridge, these five people have all been wrongly accused of horrendous crimes. Some of them, more than once.

MR S: I see. Oh dear. (*To the WRONGLY ACCUSED*). You poor fellows. I too was once –

OSCAR: Yeah, they know. (*To the WRONGLY ACCUSED*). See? Mr Surridge is on your side. He's not going to turn you away.

MR S: Of course not! You must stay as long as you wish. You're all very welcome here at TAGS. Any wrongly accused person is a friend of mine.

OSCAR: And of mine.

HENRY: Have you also been wrongly accused, Oscar?

OSCAR: Well…(*laughs modestly*) I spend most of my time in a school, so…obviously yes. I had a detention every night last term, for lying. Only I *wasn't* lying. The new French teacher really was a clay model dressed up in French-looking clothes, not a real person. Everything he said was a recorded message.

WENDY: (*runs to the centre of the stage.*) Welcome to stay? Did he really say that we're welcome to stay?

GEORGE: You spoke! You're speaking!

DANNY: Yes, he did say it. I think he meant it too.

HENRY: This is unbelievable!

GEORGE: In the light of this extraordinary turn of events – someone declaring himself willing to give us a chance – I propose that we immediately adopt a 'Can Do' attitude, and do our very best to give advice in the manner of people's heroes, to the full extent of our ability.

SERENA: I agree.

WENDY: I'll try, but it's going to be tough.

HENRY: So, so tough.

DANNY: We're all suffering from complex post-traumatic stress disorder.

GEORGE: No one who has never been wrongly accused of a serious crime can begin to imagine how terrible it is.

SONG NO. 13: BALLAD OF THE WRONGLY ACCUSED

WENDY sings:

Doesn't matter if you did it,
Doesn't matter what you say.
No-one cares if you're acquitted.
No one cares if on the day
That a murder was committed
On a street in Gamlingay,
You were eating a burrito
In a bar in Santa Fe.

Pretty soon you lose your house;
Shortly afterwards, your car.
There's a hundred different hashtags
For how gross they think you are.
Everybody in New Mexico
Swears you were in that bar.
Still, you're banished from the garden centre
And the cinema.

Everyone has their suspicions,
Their opinions and their thoughts.
They don't care how juries vote
Or what goes on in courts.

They petition to exclude you
From all parties, treats and sports
And you're banned alike from betting shops
And five star luxury resorts.

Former friends soon start to cut you
Out of every photograph.
Next you're urged to find a victim
Of a crime, and give him half
Of your pension and life savings,
And then take him on as staff,
And you can't get served in shops without
A face-concealing scarf,

So you're treated like a monster,
And you fear it must be true,
When your mum and dad say, 'Darling
We trust everyone but you.'
How are we supposed to take this?
What are we supposed to do?
Is there any hope? Please tell us,
Oscar, can we count on you?

OSCAR: You can. You can count on me and Mr Surridge. Now, let's get to work. I'm assuming none of you has ever pretended to be someone's hero in order to give advice before?

All WRONGLY ACCUSED say that no, they haven't.

OSCAR: Then I'm going to need to train you, and myself, quickly. We've already got a queue halfway round the block for our new Tribute Advice-Giving Service.

MR S: Have we? How?

OSCAR: Online ads. Lead magnets, funnels, landing pages…we've got it *all* going on.

MR S: What…what does any of that mean?

OSCAR: It means… (*Rolls his eyes*) Never mind. We've got more important things to get on with. Let's start the training with a role play. (*Goes over to GEORGE and brings him into the middle of the stage.*) Right, you're going to be the hero. Mr Surridge, you be the customer. Think of a hero someone might ask for.

MR S: Um… er… how about Alfred Hitchcock, the movie director?

OSCAR: (*to GEORGE*) D'you reckon you could pretend to be Alfred Hitchcock?

GEORGE: Yes.

OSCAR: Go on, then.

GEORGE: Um… (*Thinks. Then says confidently/arrogantly*) I need a beautiful blonde woman for my next movie, and I need her right now. And… a shower curtain!

OSCAR: Brilliant! This is totally going to work.

HENRY: But if we're offering advice… I mean, what sort of advice might Alfred Hitchcock give? I'm not sure I'd know.

Everyone looks at GEORGE.

GEORGE: Um…I firmly believe that there's no problem that can't be solved by…(*thinks hard*)…a beautiful blonde. Or a shower curtain.

OSCAR: No, no, no. (*Shakes his head*) That's not what Alfred Hitchcock would say.

GEORGE: How do you know?

OSCAR: He's more likely to give normal advice, isn't he? Appropriate to the situation. I mean, whoever you're pretending to be, if someone asks you what to do about a blocked drain, you'd probably tell them to try using a plunger.

HENRY: He's right!

SERENA: Yes, heroes don't stop being regular people.

DANNY: A blocked drain looks the same to a famous genius as it does to your average man or woman on the street.

OSCAR: Okaaaay…that's enough descent into full-blown communism for one day. Let's get you all properly trained, so that we can open our doors to new opportunities and new customers!

Lights go down.

SCENE 6

TAGS staff ANNIE, PAUL, JEN and CATHY are in the home of KAREN BEATON, host of the 'Justice for Locked Room Luke' podcast.

KAREN: I'm not denying that Derek Surridge has been a decent boss since he opened his…adhesive gels establishment. I'm sure he has. Why wouldn't he want to…give back to the world, once he's been fortunate enough to get away such a terrible crime? I'm sure that's how he sees it. He's grateful for his second chance, no doubt. In my view that makes him even more of a monster.

GRACE: But he really isn't. He's kind and thoughtful.

KAREN: (*annoyed to be contradicted*) Do you honestly believe I would accuse him of the kidnap and murder of his son in every single episode of my hugely popular 'Justice for Locked Room Luke' podcast if I were not sure of his guilt? Ask yourselves this: why hasn't Surridge taken legal action against me? If he's innocent, my podcast is full of slander against him.

LEO: What makes you so sure he did it?

KAREN: He lied to the police. Witnesses saw him driving out of the school car park with Luke sitting beside him in the car. Yet he flat out denied it.

MOLLY: Perhaps the witnesses were mistaken.

KAREN: (after a short pause) If you must know… *I* was the witness in question. That's how I know. I saw Luke Surridge as clearly as I'm seeing you now. I knew his face very well; my son was in his class at Pffisham. Luke was often at our house. And he was *definitely* in that car, sitting right next to his father. I don't know how, but Surridge must have gone straight to the Detention Unit after his meeting with the head and…set Luke free. Only to kidnap him away from his mother and murder him. (*She shudders.*)

LEO: Wait. You didn't see Mr Surridge actually kill Luke, did you?

KAREN: (*irritated to have her expertise questioned*) Well, no, but–

GRACE: Then you can't know that he did that. Maybe Luke's not dead. Maybe he's absolutely fine.

KAREN: Don't be naive. You're as bad as the police! They stopped taking me seriously the moment I told them… (*stops suddenly*)

LEO: Go on.

KAREN: No. This conversation is over. I'd like you to leave now, please.

MOLLY: (*Stands up*) If you really want us to go, then we will. But… Oscar has told us a bit about Inspector Oliver Coode and his colleague, Sergeant Wilderspin. He says they're both as dumb as a big pile of bricks.

KAREN: Well…(*slightly mollified*) I don't know who this Oscar person is, but he's dead right.

MOLLY: In that case…(*musters all her courage*) it's not true what you said, about us being as bad as the police. Because we're not dumb. Some of us are quite bright.

KAREN: Very well, then, if you really want to know: Inspector Coode believed me at first when I said I'd seen Surridge driving away from Pffisham with Luke in his car. It all started to go wrong when he asked for a full description, everything I remembered, and…well, at first I told him that both Derek Surridge and Luke were wearing blue and white striped pyjamas.

GRACE: Pyjamas?

LEO and MOLLY gasp.

KAREN: (*nods*) I described them meticulously, thinking I was helping: white with thick navy stripes. But the inspector said I was being ridiculous, that no one wears pyjamas in the daytime, and especially not to a meeting with a school headteacher. And the trouble was, the head confirmed that Derek Surridge was wearing normal clothes, and so why on earth would he suddenly be in pyjamas?

MOLLY: And so the police decided you must be wrong?

KAREN: (*nods, sighing*) I then damaged my own credibility even further by getting flustered and saying that maybe I'd got mixed up and Luke was the only one in pyjamas – at which point Inspector Coode announced triumphantly that Luke had been wearing his school uniform when he was locked in the Detention Unit…and I ended up looking like a fool who didn't know what she was talking about. Tell me, why did you all react so…strongly when I said 'pyjamas'? Have you…(*leans forward as a suspicion starts to form*) Have any of you seen Derek Surridge wearing pyjamas in the daytime?

TAGS staff exchange guilty looks but say nothing.

KAREN: (*shocked*) But...if you have, you must go straight to the police and tell them! Don't you see? Your silence, your so-called loyalty...it might be protecting a murderer!

SCENE 7

TAGS staff ANNIE, PAUL, JEN and CATHY are at Pffisham School interviewing GWEN LAPP, who is holding a big iron key. They're all standing outside the Detention Unit.

PAUL: So, if we could get a video clip of you unlocking the door, or locking it, that would be great!

GWEN L: I'm afraid that's quite impossible. We've currently got a most unruly and savage pupil contained in there – Tobias Boland. Known as ASBO by his friends, which tells you all you need to know. I've got a better idea: why don't you take a photo of me smiling and holding the key next to lock?

CATHY: No, we really do need a video clip. It's the satisfying clank of the key turning in the lock that we want, you see.

GWEN L: But…(*confused*)…I thought you said *Prison Design Weekly* was a glossy magazine. How are you going to put a video clip in a printed publication?

JEN: Yes, but there's a huge online readership too, Mrs Lapp. You wouldn't want them to miss out, would you? Think of all the adoring fans you'll soon have, all over the world… from Aberystwyth to Arizona.

GWEN L: Arizona! (*Her face lights up*) Pima County, Arizona, is my favourite place in the world.

PAUL: There you go then.

GWEN L: But the security risk…

ANNIE: Don't worry. Just unlock the door and then immediately lock it again. That won't give ASBO any time to escape. Paul, start the camera now.

PAUL: Okay…filming… Whenever you're ready, Mrs Lapp.

As GWEN LAPP unlocks the door, ANNIE, CATHY and JEN grab her and pull her to one side, pushing her up against the wall. The door opens wide to reveal ASBO slumped over the table in there, the green chicken on a plate in front of him, still uneaten.

ANNIE: Quick, ASBO, run. We've been sent by Oscar to set you free.

ASBO: (*Stands up, leisurely. Stretches.*) My *man,* Oscar! Get *in*!

ANNIE: No, get out! Now!

TAGS STAFF let go of GWEN LAPP, but she can't move away from the wall. She's stuck to it. She struggles to break free, but fails.

PAUL: You won't be able to stop him from leaving, Mrs Lapp. We've stuck you to the wall with one of our strongest adhesive gels. Cathy spread it all over the back of your dress while I was explaining about the reach and readership of *Prison Design Weekly* – which doesn't exist, by the way.

GWEN L: (*snarls*) You treacherous creatures! You'll burn in hell for this!

ASBO: Where's Oscar now?

MOLLY: He's at TAGS in town. He told us to tell you go there immediately. He's got a brand new iPhone for you, just like he promised, and he also needs you to start being someone's hero. Like, straight away.

ASBO: (*puzzled but intrigued and pleased*) Cool beans.

ASBO saunters off, and TAGS staff follow, leaving GWEN LAPP stuck to the wall, struggling to detach herself.

SCENE 8

Outside TAGS offices. New sign says 'TRIBUTE ADVICE GIVING SERVICE'. ADVICE SEEKERS and PEOPLE IN QUEUE are talking. LIZZIE has a wound on her finger and has wrapped it in tissue paper.

IZZY: What did you do to your finger?

LIZZIE: Nearly sliced it off with a bread-knife. It's been bleeding ever since. That's why I'm here. I need to know what to do. I was going to ring the NHS helpline, but then I saw an advert for TAGS on Facebook and I thought…what could be more amazing than getting advice from someone pretending to be my all-time hero?

GINA: Who *is* your all-time hero?

LIZZIE: Aaron Sorkin.

BILL: Who's that?

SIMON: Isn't he the creator of *The West Wing*?

BILL: What's *The West Wing*?

ZENA: It's some lame TV show.

LIZZIE: Actually, it's the best TV show ever. Philistine! Who's your hero? Someone pathetic, no doubt.

ZENA: Actually, it's Elvis Presley – who, I *think* you'll find, is the King of Rock and Roll and not pathetic at all.

BILL: My hero's Alfred Hitchcock. I specifically want advice about beautiful blondes and shower curtains.

SIMON: Me too. What a massive coincidence! Shall we share the advice and split the cost? (*He and Bill shake hands.*)

IZZY: Wow. I can't believe how shallow you all are. I have two heroes, and both are properly admirable people. I'm going to pay double to get advice from both of them.

GINA: Who are they?

IZZY: (*in a superior tone*) You probably haven't heard of them. One is Marie Curie, the scientist, and the other is Steven Biko, the South African freedom fighter. There was a film made about his struggle against Apartheid: *Cry Freedom*, it was called.

SIMON: Are you from South Africa?

IZZY: No. I'm from Little Shelford.

Enter DUNCAN SURRIDGE

DUNCAN: A warm welcome to all of you…problem-bearing people! Do come in. Wait! Not all of you at once. Only four of your…um…*heroes* are ready. (*Mutters, facing away from them*) This is so absurd, I can't believe it's going to work.

LIZZIE: Is my hero ready? Oh, please, say he is!

DUNCAN: Are you here to see Steven the South African chap?

LIZZIE: No.

DUNCAN: Elvis Presley?

ZENA: That's me!

DUNCAN: In you go, then.

Exit ZENA, running enthusiastically.

DUNCAN: Who's here for Aaron Sorkin, creator of TV show *The West Wing*?

LIZZIE: That's me!

Exit LIZZIE, running enthusiastically.

IZZY: I'm here to see 'Steven the South African chap', as you so ignorantly call him. And Marie Curie.

DUNCAN: If you must. I mean…you do know that Marie Curie is a charity, don't you? Not an actual person?

IZZY: (*laughs*) Step aside, fool. I don't mean to be rude, but how are you not unemployed?

Exit IZZY.

DUNCAN: (*to GINA*) Unbelievable. The temerity! You try to help people…

GINA: I'm here to see Mary, Queen of Scots.

DUNCAN: Before or after she had her head…Never mind. In you go.

Exit GINA, running enthusiastically

DUNCAN: Oh, adhesive gels, I miss you!

SCENE 9

TAGS offices, interior. OSCAR and MR SURRIDGE are standing to one side. The WRONGLY ACCUSED are standing in a line, waiting to be consulted. GEORGE is Aaron Sorkin, DANNY is Steven Biko, HENRY is Elvis Presley, WENDY is Alfred Hitchcock, SERENA is Mary, Queen of Scots. They are all sitting below signs with their 'Hero' names on them, to make clear who is who. Enter LIZZIE, IZZY, GINA and ZENA.

OSCAR: Fingers crossed, Mr Surridge. Our first customers. If they're happy with the advice they get, they'll tell everyone they know, and word will spread. TAGS might be worth a billion dollars by Christmas. Definitely worth me staying on, wasn't it? I'll have been here three weeks tomorrow – I can't believe it's gone so quickly.

MR S: A billion dollars. Do you really think so?

OSCAR: Trust. (*He nods at the WRONGLY ACCUSED*) Mo' life to da young tugs.

MR S: I'm not sure I understand what that means, but…it sounds nice!

Enter ASBO, climbing in through an open window.

ASBO: Oscar. Yo!

OSCAR: (*Joyful*) Faa-am! Blud's freeeeee!

OSCAR and ASBO perform a weird Reprobates gang hand gesture.

ASBO: Wha' gwan? Where's my new iPhone at?

OSCAR: No time to explain now, mate – I'll fill you in later, and give you the phone too. For now…stand here and pretend to be Marie Curie, some leng ting who helped cure cancer. (*He places a big sign saying 'Marie Curie' above ASBO's head.*)

ASBO: Sweet.

OSCAR: Okay, everyone. Let's do this. (*Whispers to MR S*) Ssh, listen…

SONG NO. 14: IF I CUT MY FINGER

LIZZIE sings:

If I cut my finger
Should I go to a doctor,
Or just put on a plaster?
Which would cure it faster?
Tell me, Aaron Sorkin.
Give me the help I'm needing.
The sooner you start talkin',
The sooner I stop bleeding.

Shall I rinse it underneath the cold tap
Like my mother always said I should
Or will that do me no good at all?
Shall I wrap a sock around it,
Ultra-violet ultrasound it?
Oh, how hard I've tried
But never with the man who wrote
The West Wing *on my side.*

IZZY sings:

If a baby pigeon
Is living in my roof void
And I hear his wings beating,
Loud as central heating,
Tell me, Steven Biko,
Tell me, Marie Curie –
Tolerant and eco,
Or wreck his nest in fury?

Shall I rinse him underneath the cold tap
Like my mother never said I should
Or will that do him no good at all?
Shall I wrap my arms around him,
Name him and be glad I found him?
Did either of you get
The chance to have a Little Shelford pigeon as a pet?

GINA and ZENA sing alternate lines:

If I'm feeling bloated / If I take some small change
Uncomfortable and swollen / From the office slush fund
Should I lay off dairy? / Is that a bit embezzle-y?
Tell me Scots Queen Mary. / Help me, Elvis Presley.

LIZZIE, IZZY, GINA and ZENA sing:

Will you give us sound advice for ever?
We're so lucky to stand next to you.
Without you, we would be no good at all.
Wrap your wisest words around us.

We're much better since you found us.
Oh, how hard we've tried
But everybody needs their favourite hero by their side.

If I cut my finger.
If I cut my finger…

A phone on a nearby desk starts to ring, as WRONGLY ACCUSED and ADVICE SEEKERS exit, leaving only OSCAR, MR SURRIDGE and ASBO. OSCAR answers the phone.

OSCAR: Hello, you've reached Tribute Advice-Giving Service. Oscar Landrigan speaking. No, this isn't Mr Surridge. That's why I said, 'Oscar Landrigan speaking'. I'm his right hand man. No…no, you're right, I don't really work here. I'm just a temporary Terrible Boy using his unofficially extended work experience placement to make risky and controversial changes. What do you mean, you know who I am? Cathy, is that you? Cathy from TAGS? Well, why didn't you say so? You're scared of phone calls. I see. (*Sighs*) What? Yes, I know you've broken ASBO out. He's here. Haha. I wish I could have seen that. Describe it to me. Include every detail… (*long pause*) Excellent. And…have you heard from the others yet? What did they say? Did they manage to get anything interesting out of Karen Beaton from the 'Justice for Locked Room Luke' podcast?….I see. (*Very long pause*) Really? That's… fascinating. Wait, stop. I've got a crucial question for you, Cathy. Please think carefully before answering because this really matters. Hello? (*Shakes the phone*) Hello? Cathy? Ah, Paul. Right, of course, Cathy's scared of crucial questions. I'll ask you, then: when you let ASBO out of the detention unit, was there anything or anyone else inside the room with him? Okay, a green chicken breast on a tray. A table… Nothing else? No. I see. Thank you, Paul. (*Turns to MR SURRIDGE, a triumphant expression on his face*) I *think*… Mr Surridge, I reckon I've solved the mystery! I think I know exactly what happened to your son, Luke. And if I'm right, then it's good news. It means Luke is alive and well, and I should be able to find him quite easily.

MR S: What? Are you being serious, Oscar? Please, do not joke about something so painful.

OSCAR: I'm being very serious. I just need to ask ASBO a few quick questions…

OSCAR and ASBO withdraw to a corner for a private, whispered exchange. At the end of this, ASBO puts out his hand and we see OSCAR giving him a new iPhone. ASBO looks thrilled, hugs OSCAR and then kisses the phone. Then OSCAR walks back over to MR SURRIDGE.

OSCAR: My suspicions have been confirmed. You and your son will soon be officially reunited, Mr Surridge.

MR S: Then…if we're going to find Luke… (*Pauses, thinking*) Duncan! Diane!

Enter DUNCAN and DIANE

MR S: Both of you, leave with Oscar at once. Help him to retrieve my poor Luke from…wherever he is.

OSCAR: (*to MR SURRIDGE*) Don't *you* want to come with me?

MR S: I do, but I can't. I'm in my pyjamas.

OSCAR: (*knowingly*) And you'd never go outside wearing your pyjamas, would you? You'd never, for instance, be wearing pyjamas anywhere near Pffisham School?

MR S: What a bizarre suggestion!

OSCAR: You would also never allow Luke to go to school wearing pyjamas – am I right?

MR S: Of course I wouldn't. What do you take me for?

OSCAR: (*Nods happily*) It's all coming together nicely. Karen Beaton, host of the 'Justice for Locked Room Luke' podcast, was dead wrong about you–

MR S: (*emphatically, outraged*) Yes, she was!

OSCAR: – but she wan't *lying*. There's an important difference.

MR S: Whatever do you mean, Oscar?

OSCAR: Never mind. That's a discussion for later. Finding Luke comes first.

MR S: Indeed. Of course. Well…off you go, then!

OSCAR: Come with me, Mr Surridge. I mean…just because you're in your pyjamas *now*, that doesn't mean you must always remain in your pyjamas. Don't you think that, for the momentous occasion of finding your long lost son, you might…y'know. Get dressed?

MR S: Dressed? In…in day clothes? (*Rubs his chin, thinking*) Yes. Yes, I think the time has come! Diane, bring me a suitable outfit – the kind people wear to go outside. Oscar…you have so many brilliant ideas. I can hardly keep up with you. You're a marvel. Tribute Advice-Giving Service! Me getting dressed! Genius! Once all this is over and Luke has been safely returned, I want you to stay here and continue working with us all at New TAGS for as long as possible.

SONG NO. 15: THAT WORKS FOR ME

MR SURRIDGE sings:

You don't work here, don't get paid.
When you should have left, you stayed.
You've made changes you weren't authorised to make.
Neither boss nor employee,
You transformed the company
And presumably you did it for the sake
Of improving something flawed.
That was your entire reward
And you never asked for thanks or asked for more
And not once did you resent
All the wages that were spent
On the people who could not see what you saw,

And now, from where I'm standing
It appears we have new branding –
A new angle, a new purpose, and our bank account's
expanding.
Well, if all of this is true
(As of right now, it seems to be),
You could stay a month or two
Or a year or two or three?
Oscar, if that works for you,
Well, then, that works for me.

DIANE and DUNCAN sing:

Mr Surridge, you'll regret this.
Have you gone completely crazy?
Are we now supposed to let this
Useless schoolboy who's been lazy
All his life until he came here
March around as if he's made it?
He must be the one to blame here.
Can't you see the way he's played it?

MR SURRIDGE sings:

All I see from where I'm standing
Is a company that's thriving
And some jealous people landing
Spiteful blows, and also skiving,
And if all of this is true
(As of right now, it seems to be),
He can stay a month or two
Or a year, or two or three.
Oscar, if that works for you
Well, then, that works for me.

OSCAR sings:

I think I should stick with you
And I think this company
Still has important work to do
To be the best that it can be,
So I'll stay a month or two
Or a year or two or three.
If you're sure that works for you?
Well, then, that works for me.

DIANE, DUNCAN and MR SURRIDGE sing:

And if all of this is true
(As of right now, it seems to be)
You can stay a month or two
Or a year or two or three…
Now we've seen what you can do
How amazing it would be
If we all can work with you –
Well, then, that works for me.

Enter BETHANY VOSS

BETH: Oscar! Oh, Oscar, come quickly. Something terrible's happened.

He follows her outside.

SCENE 10

Outside TAGS. OSCAR and BETHANY are standing to the side as hundreds of people wanting TAGS's advice are queuing round the block.

OSCAR: What's happened?

BETH: Two unspeakably awful things: first of all…there's a strange new virus that's been named after a Spanish beer and it's killing people all over the world.

OSCAR: *What*?

BETH: Apparently all the schools in the UK are shutting down. Immediately! Including Pffisham School!

OSCAR lets out a triumphant cheer. Then he drops to his knees, puts his hands together in prayer and mouths 'Yes! Thank you, Lord! Thank you!'

BETH: No, Oscar, it's terrible news. It means Bartie and I will miss out on the chance to become even cleverer than we already are. And you and I won't be able to see each other ever again.

OSCAR: Why not? We can see each other outside school.

BETH: We can't, though, because no one's allowed to go to anyone else's house either.

OSCAR: No one'll obey that rule. It's insane. Everyone knows that people who make insane rules are just crying out, subconsciously, to have them broken. (*Proud expression*) That's where I come in. (*He frowns*) Actually, come to think of it,

I might have heard Mum and Dad discussing this weird virus thing last night. I'm pretty sure I heard Mum say, 'I'm going to carry on doing exactly what I want, Peter, and no one can stop me!'

BETH: My parents are saying the opposite: that we all have to obey the government and I have to obey them – Mum and Dad. Which includes… (*She sighs*) They're telling me I have to break up with you, Oscar. That we can't be engaged any more. Bartie tried to persuade them to be happy for us, but…he failed. And Mum and Dad are very upset about that too, because now Bartie isn't as all-round successful as he used to be.

OSCAR: Don't worry. I'll persuade your parents. They don't realise it yet, but I'm irresistible. (*He grins.*) Beth, it's all going to be fine. Your mum and dad will be thrilled we're together by the time I've finished with them!

SCENE 11

Enter NARRATOR, GWEN LAPP, FRANK and PAMOLYN VOSS and camera crews, journalists etc. They are followed onto the stage by other Pffisham School staff, students, parents, TAGS staff, as many cast members as can fit on stage.

NARR: 18th of March. The education secretary, Gavin Williamson, has today announced that, once schools close on Friday, they will remain shut until further notice. All over the country, teenagers who enjoyed jumping through the hoops required by an ineffective, failing, creatively stifling system are heartbroken. Teachers are especially worried about those pupils who were meant to be taking their GCSEs and A-levels this year, and most schools have accepted that they will have to switch to an online learning model for the time being. Only one headteacher, Mrs Gwen Lapp of Pffisham School in Cambridge, has attempted to defy the ruling and keep her school open, claiming that…

GWEN L: We at Pffisham are experts when it comes to locking pupils away in conditions of extremely healthy and safe isolation within our Detention Unit. We have applied to the government for special permission to remain open, based on our new turbo-charged student-imprisonment model, which I introduced shortly after finding myself glued to a wall by hooligans who had invaded our building under false pretences. I and my staff would far rather our students endured misery, loneliness and the complete breakdown of their social lives at Pffisham School than at home, and I shall continue to lobby both the Prime Minister and the Education Secretary to this effect.

PAMOLYN VOSS steps forward, dragging her husband FRANK with her.

PAM V: My name is Pamolyn Voss, and I'm a parent of two children at Pffisham, including star pupil, Bartie Voss. My husband Frank and I fully support Mrs Lapp, and demand that the school be reopened before it has even closed.

FRANK V: We are confident that children as high-achieving as ours won't die or even come down with a sore throat as a result of any virus that affects the rest of the population. Our children are not 'most people', and obviously other people's children don't matter.

PAM V: Exactly.

NARR: The mood across the country is bleak. Reporters searched long and hard in order to find anyone who wasn't feeling terrible about everything. Eventually, however, they tracked down one group of teenagers in central Cambridge…

Enter OSCAR, ASBO, 3-STRIKE and WASPY. Each is carrying a bottle of champagne and a glass, and has colourful streamers from party-poppers around his/her neck.

NARR: …who seemed to be in distinctly celebratory spirits. When asked if they weren't concerned about their exam grades, their spokesperson, Oscar Landrigan, said…

SONG NO. 16 – HERE'S TO YOU, GAVIN WILLIAMSON

OSCAR sings:

It's not about the grades.
It's about the education.
Who needs formal accolades?
What we need is information.
I never knew there was such a thing as
A Secretary of State for Education.
Today I learned that we have one
And that his name's Gavin Williamson.

He's closed down all the schools, he's
Cancelled every examination.
He's made a whole new set of rules
After some careful deliberation, and
Some kids my age, crazy fools,
See this as cause for commiseration.
Of their number, I'm not one.

(*OSCAR raises a glass*)

Here's to you, Gavin Williamson.

And unlike the famous song, I do like Mondays
And all four other days that used to make me wanna run.
No more Pffisham School, so no more hopes-and-dreams-undone days.
Monday's gonna be my favourite one,
The perfect day to say, 'Hooray, a whole new week's begun!'
And this week is gonna be a sensation,
Thanks to you, Gavin Williamson.

No more teachers telling me
They find my posture intimidating.
Give me a random GCSE
In Politics or Rollerskating.
Geography, Sociology,
So never-endingly aggravating –
Watch them vanish one by one
Thanks to you, Gavin Williamson.

And unlike the famous song, I now like Mondays.
Mondays just became the new best friends of Oscar Landrigan.
No more searching-for-a-silver-lining, never-finding-one days.
I'll spend the morning on my PlayStation
Then order lunch (thank you, Deliveroo) from Chosen Bun,
And I'll be free from punishment and persecution
Thanks to you, Gavin Williamson.

Yeah, unlike the famous song, I so love Mondays –
Life's as good as Prison Break *when they escape in Season 1.*
No more five-in-a-row, dead-on-arrival hit and run days.
My mum says I should read And Then There Were None –
She thinks I'll finally get myself a decent education
And it's goodbye to the old, abysmal simulation,
Thanks to you, Gavin Williamson.
It's all thanks to you, Gavin Williamson.

All exit, apart from NARRATOR.

NARR: This isn't the first time Oscar Landrigan has made the news. Last year he achieved notoriety by helping an amateur detective by the name of John Danes, aka The Generalist, solve two murders, including that of Oscar's late grandmother, the best-selling romantic novelist Harriet Landrigan. Asked to comment on her son's cavalier attitude to his formal education, Oscar's mother Clemency Landrigan said…

CLEM: (*voiceover*) No one ever taught him anything at that dump of a school anyway. All they ever did was find excuses to lock him up in the Detention Unit, under the supervision of Monsieur LeClay who wasn't even a person, let alone a French teacher. He was a clay model, as Oscar proved when he chopped off his clay arm! And *still* the school didn't release him – in fact, they kept him locked up for longer. They punished him for revealing the truth. If it were up to me, Pffisham School would remain closed forever. It presents a far greater danger to children than any lethal virus ever could.

SCENE 12

OSCAR is sitting in the living room of the VOSS family. He is at one end of the room, looking normal in jeans, trainers and a hoody. At the far end of the room, behind a freestanding pane of thick glass, are FRANK, PAMOLYN and BETHANY VOSS, all wearing masks and sanitising their hands with sprays and cloths.

OSCAR: ...and that was how I worked out where Luke Surridge was. We found him alive and well, just as I promised Mr Surridge we would. And bear in mind, this was after I turned a failing business full of utter wimps into a massively profitable operation – even more so now that we've moved online. Now we can serve customers all over the world. This lockdown's been an incredible opportunity for us. And don't forget, it was thanks to me that a significant number of wrongly accused people were able to find meaning in life once again and have a second chance. And those wimps I mentioned? Not wimps any more, not after they took a risk and helped me free ASBO and solve the Luke Surridge mystery. They proved to themselves that they were capable of *so* much more than selling glue to the same old customers day in day out. So...all in all, what I'm trying to tell you is that, despite being a little... unconventional in my approach to life, I'm actually quite an impressive character. I think I could massively add value to the Voss family if you'd open your minds a bit. And Mrs Voss, may I say...that painting on the wall behind you is stunning. Is it one of yours? Beth tells me you're an artist. I'd love to see more of your pictures, if I may?

PAM: (*pulls off her mask*) How *dare* you abbreviate my daughter's name! She's called Bethany! And I don't believe you found Luke Surridge. There's been nothing on the news.

OSCAR: That's right. Mr Surridge decided he wants it kept quiet for now. I shouldn't have told you, really, but...well, I want us to get off on a good footing, with no secrets between us. Look, Mr and Mrs Voss...Bethany and I have something we'd like to tell you, something we're excited about.

PAM: (*holds up a hand to block his words*) Please don't. We've already been told, by Bartie. The first time was bad enough.

FRANK: Yes, we're somewhat ahead of you, Oscar.

SONG NO. 17: SON-IN-LAW

PAM sings:

We've heard the news. So, you've proposed to her...

OSCAR: Well, that wasn't quite how it...

PAM sings:

And she's said yes. The wedding's June next year.

OSCAR: What? No, I don't think–

BETH: (*Takes off her mask*) That's right. June.

PAM sings:

And now, no doubt, you've come to us to hear
How thrilled we both must be, and how there's nothing we'd prefer.
Well, I will not insult you with a lie.

There are some things that I would choose before
I'd choose to have you as my son-in-law,
And I will tell you what those are,
And I will tell you why…

I'd rather set fire to my eyes and hair,
Get disembowelled at noon in Market Square
Or suffocate beneath a concrete floor
Than have you, Oscar, as my son-in-law.
You're not my son-in-law.

Some foolish mothers think they can control
Their grown-up child's behaviour. I won't try.
If I succeeded, if she did comply,
That kind of intervention breeds resentment on the whole.
Still, there are realms in which I reign supreme:
Inside my heart and home, I shall express
My true opinion of this wretched mess,
The vast gulf I perceive between this nightmare and love's dream…

I'd rather chew a furious swarm of bees
Or take a knife and slice off both my knees,
Or live through never-ending nuclear war
Than have you, Oscar, as my son-in-law.
You're not my son-in-law.

OSCAR: Right. How about you, Mr Voss? I hope I can rely on you for a more positive assessment of the situation.

FRANK sings:

I'd eat the feet of fifteen stinky men
Before I'd have you in my home again.

I'd rather get my tongue trapped in a door
Than have you, Oscar, as my son-in-law.

PAM sings:

I'd rather see my whole life's work destroyed,
Obliterated by an asteroid.
Extinct as every single dinosaur
Than have you, Oscar, as my son-in-law
And I would rather tell you fair and square
Than be polite and act like I don't care,
And now that I've explained at length, I hope you know the score:
I do not want you, Oscar Landrigan,
To be my son-in-law.

OSCAR: I see. Well, I appreciate your honesty, even if this didn't go quite the way I hoped. (*Stands up to leave, makes his way to the door.*)

BETH: Oscar, don't leave! Change their minds!

PAM: Please *do* leave.

FRANK: (*yells*) Yes, get out and don't come back. Do your bit for public health by staying at home in the mansion that used to belong to your trashy romantic-pot-boiler-writing grandmother and forget all about the nineteen thousand pounds in Bethany's ISA that you're desperate to get your grubby hands on.

OSCAR: (*patiently, takes deep breath*) For the last time…I'm a multi-millionaire. I don't care about nineteen thousand pounds. Goodbye, Beth. If being with you means putting up with these fun-sponge dickheads for the rest of my life, I don't think I can do it. I'm sorry.

(*He leaves the house and, as he's walking down the street, FRED CROFT appears from number 1, the house with a grey brick facade and a red door.*)

FRED: (*eagerly*) Is it over between you and Bethany? I heard shouting.

OSCAR: You must be Fred Croft. I believe my relationship with Beth is over, yes.

FRED: (*frostily*) Her name is Bethany.

OSCAR: She hates it, though. She told me to call her Beth. Names can change, you know. Look…

(*OSCAR pulls a Sharpie out of his trouser pocket and scribbles over the 'Alpha' bit of Alpha Avenue on the street sign. He writes 'Enemy' instead, so the sign reads 'Enemy Avenue'.*)

OSCAR: (*walking away*) Bye-bye Freddy-Fred-Fred. Enjoy your future on this street where you live: Enemy Avenue, with your monstrous future in-laws.

SCENE 13

CLEMENCY LANDRIGAN is on her phone at Idlewyld House, home of the Landrigan family.

CLEM: What do you mean? But…surely not again? I can't believe that's possible…Well, no, I'm not saying you're wrong, but…well, it's most unfair, that's all.

Enter OSCAR

CLEM: (*angrily*) It's corruption, pure and simple. It shouldn't be allowed. Goodbye. (*She tosses her phone onto a nearby sofa.*)

OSCAR: No, it shouldn't be allowed – if you're talking about parents ruining their children's lives.

CLEM: Darling! When have I ever ruined your life?

OSCAR: I'm not talking about you. I meant Pam and Frank Voss. Never mind. (*With determination*) Luckily, I don't need Beth Voss in my life in order to be happy. I only need me on my own side and I'll be fine. (*Sounding increasingly doubtful*) I'm going to find myself someone much better. Or at least, someone with parents who don't hate me. (*Sighs*) I did really like Bethany, though. And Bartie's okay too. (*To CLEM, suddenly curious*) What were you talking about, on the phone?

CLEM: Oh, only the stupid International Perfume Society Awards. They've given the prizes to all the same people they give them to every year – Byredo and Jo bloody Malone! I don't know why I bother! Do you know what, Oscar? If TAGS wasn't currently closed thanks to this wretched virus, I'd go there myself, right now, and demand advice from someone pretending to be my all-time hero. Advice about whether to give up perfume-making and start doing something quite different instead.

OSCAR: Who is your all-time hero?

CLEM: Gosh, that's a good question. I hadn't thought that far ahead. Do you know what, darling? I think it might be you!

OSCAR: Don't be silly. I'm your son.

CLEM: Yes, but I think it's true. And I don't believe it's just my maternal bias, either. Think about it, Oscar: you're fifteen years old and you've already helped to solve two murders and been the brains behind a multi-million-pound reinvention of a local business. And you set ASBO free from that dreadful room where the revolting Gwen Lapp was effectively starving him to death.

OSCAR: And I found Luke Surridge, don't forget.

CLEM: Well...you *say* you did, but...

OSCAR: (*groans*) Mum, how many times? When he's ready, Mr Surridge will hold a big press conference and explain everything. I wouldn't lie about something as important as Luke being found. (*Thoughtfully*) The truth is...thanks to first John Danes, and then Mr Surridge, and then the Wrongly Accused and...well, just all the inspiring people I've known... Thanks to all of them, I'm no longer the same woeful reprobate that I once was.

CLEM: Oh, darling… Well, you know I've always thought you were super duper in every way.

OSCAR: (*emphatically, as if CLEM doesn't know quite how vital a point she's made*) I *do* know that, yes. That, I believe, was a key ingredient of what turned out to be my eventual amazingness. (*Frowns*) The trouble is, not all people have even one parent who loves them unconditionally and thinks they're fantastic even when they act like a dick. And that's a problem. That's a *big* problem for this damaged world we live in. Hmmm. (*Pondering*)

CLEM: (*gasps*) Oscar! I've just had a brilliant idea! TAGS can't give face-to-face advice at the moment because of the lock-down, but what about the digital arm of the operation? I could go online and ask for someone pretending to be you, my hero, to give me some wise counsel.

OSCAR: Or you could just ask the real me, who's right in front of you?

CLEM: (*claps her hands together, delighted*) Oh, how ingenious! John Danes always said you were ingenious and he was jolly well right.

OSCAR: This is my point. When The Generalist said that about me, I asked myself, 'What if he's right?' That was the beginning of me starting to think of me in that way, which was what set me off on the path to making it a reality. That's the only reason I was able to solve the mystery of missing Luke Surridge – because I decided to believe that I was the only person who could.

CLEM: So you're saying that...you believing it made it come true? I'm not sure that's *quite* how the world works, darling...

OSCAR: I am. Most people don't realise you can just decide who you want to be and then be it. I never thought I'd see ASBO become a really convincing Marie Curie...and then I did. Obviously I never met the real Marie Curie, but there's no doubt in my mind that ASBO was a better one. The point is, we can reinvent ourselves whenever we want to, Mum. You don't have to be a perfume designer any more if there's something you'd rather do. Change your self-concept first, and everything else will follow.

SONG NO. 18: FIND YOU (OSCAR'S VERSION)

OSCAR sings:

I thought I was stuck at war with school –
All I could do was hate, and break most of the rules,
And to be fair to me, that was how life used to be,
But then new opportunities arose,
So trust that those

Will find you, find you,
Coming up behind you –
Seize them, pursue them,
Just be open to them...
They will find you,
Find you,
Don't let doubters blind you.
You can win here
All you need is to begin here,

In this place, exactly where you are.
Embrace the present circumstance and you'll go far.
Aiming high, it helps to know
That you were never starting low.
Your dreams already see where you could be,
And if you're like me

They'll find you, find you…
Coming up behind you…

CLEM sings:

You can achieve it.
All you need is to believe it.

OSCAR sings:

They'll find you, find you.
I'll be right behind you,
Bound for glory

CLEM and OSCAR sing:

The perfect way to live your story
Will find you,
Will find you,
Will find you,
Will find you,
Will find you.

Lights go down.

SCENE 14

Night time. BETHANY is at home, sitting hunched on the sofa, crying and wearing a COVID mask. Every so often she pulls it down around her neck to howl in anguish, then she pulls it back up again. Enter BARTIE, not wearing a mask.

BARTIE: Bethany! I've got some amazing news! Oh… What's wrong?

BETHANY says something garbled from behind her mask.

BARTIE: Take that stupid thing off! Look…I don't care what Mum and Dad say. If we die, we die. It's the only way to live.

BETH: (*Tearing off her mask and hurling it across the room*) That's such a good point, actually. I can't think why I'm trying to save my life now that it's lost all meaning.

BARTIE: What are you on about?

BETH: Oscar and I have broken up. Mum and Dad said I wasn't allowed to be engaged to him any more, so he decided to stop loving me. I watched it happen, right before my eyes. And then he left, vandalising our street sign as he went.

BARTIE: So that's why it says 'Enemy Avenue'. I did wonder.

BETH: (*wistfully*) It's something Oscar and I have always disagreed about.

BARTIE: (*sits on the sofa beside her*) How do you mean?

BETH: Oscar believes we can change our feelings at the drop of a hat, simply by thinking different thoughts. I disagree. And the tragedy is… (*she bursts into a fresh flood of tears*) he's right about him and I'm right about me. He stopped loving me on the spot, easy peasy, whereas I find it impossible to stop loving him. Cute, loyal Fred came round and said I could be his fiancée instead, but…that would be torture! I don't love Fred. I don't even care about the nineteen grand in my ISA any more. I'd happily give it all to Oscar.

BARTIE: Don't do that. Within ten minutes he'd have spent it on a lukewarm cheeseburger and some appalling, overpriced trainers. But sis, I don't understand. Did you just roll over when Mum and Dad said you had to ditch Oscar? Why didn't you stand up to them?

BETH: Because they're terrifying tyrants, that's why! They're not just strict, Bartie. They're wicked. And I've been groomed since birth to let them control every aspect of my life and think it's normal.

BARTIE: Well…yes, that's true.

BETH: (*surprised*) You agree?

BARTIE: I do – but instead of moaning about it, why not let it be the making of you? That's always been my approach.

BETH: What on earth are you talking about?

BARTIE: If you can withstand a childhood orchestrated by Pam and Frank Voss, you can survive anything. You can *do* anything. (*Nudges her, teasingly*) Ask me how I know.

BETH: How do you– Oh! Not...*Les Misérables*?

BARTIE: Yup! My plan worked. Well, mine and Oscar's. Cameron Mackintosh won. Cambridgeshire County Council lost. Thanks to a Supreme Court ruling this morning, the original version of *Les Mis* has been reinstated.

BETH: Bartie, that's brilliant. Well done you! Do you know what? I think you're right.

BARTIE: (*smug but charming*) It wouldn't be the first time.

BETH: If you can do what you've done, and if Cameron Mackintosh can... (*she leaps up*). Bartie, quick! There's no time to lose. Go and find Oscar. Tell him I choose him, not my parents. Make him come back and give me a second chance. Go now! Tell him I'm tired of being a Voss–

BARTIE: (*alarmed*) Steady on!

BETH: –and ready to become a Landrigan!

BARTIE: But...you're the one who's standing up. Can't you go?

BETH: (*does some loud, fake weeping*)

BARTIE: Oh, all right. (*Stands up and heads for the door*) Bloody girls, honestly...

BARTIE exits. BETH rushes upstairs and throws some clothes and a toothbrush into a suitcase. Once packed, she goes downstairs and outside and stands looking up at her parents' house. The moonlight shines on the two bricked-up windows on the street-facing side, and on the sign on the street corner: 'Enemy Avenue'.

SONG NO. 19: ENEMY AVENUE

BETH sings:

Once in a while, I'll tell the story
Of the way things used to be.
It's not my style
To blame it all on you, so blame it all on me.
I was a fool you could depend
Upon to be yours till the end,
Except that now it's clear
You'd never set me free.

She looks at Fred's house…

A hundred yards, another house, red door,
The front all painted grey.
The quiet facades,
What they conceal, the poor
Old price we had to pay.
My tears will fall, your heart can bleed,
But we'll survive, and first I need
To leave this jail behind and make my getaway.

Enter OSCAR from the wings…

OSCAR sings:

Enemy Avenue,
Love died here when I lost you:
The despot road, the ego's letter A.

BETH sing:

Enemy Avenue,
All the lies we tell come true.
Do you believe or understand a single word you say?

BOTH sing:

I never thought a light could shine so dark
Until I fought the fire to send a flame to save a spark.
If you think all is lost, that's never true.

OSCAR sings:

I'm bringing pure good trouble to
Enemy Avenue.

OSCAR and BETH approach each other tentatively, walking in a slow circle, neither one sure what the other is thinking…

BETH sings, looking up at her house again:

Enemy Avenue –
Plain to see, the blinded view,
Two bricked up windows, one just turned away.

OSCAR sings:

Enemy Avenue –
Time to leave for somewhere new.
Around the corner, there's a happy day…

They move closer to each other and hold hands.

BOTH sing:

I never thought a light could shine so dark
Until I fought the fire to send a flame to save a spark.
If you think all is lost, that's never true.

OSCAR sings:

My winning ways are coming to
Enemy Avenue.

PAM VOSS opens the front door.

PAM: Bethany, get inside! Now!

BETH looks at her, then back to Oscar, and sings:

Not long ago, I watched two hearts of stone
Take faith and love, and loyalty, and strip them to the bone.
They pray that I'll forget. I never do.

OSCAR sings:

I will be waiting here for you
However long I'm having to,
On Enemy Avenue.

BETH: You don't have to wait any more Oscar. I'm here, and I'm ready. Take me with you. Where are we going?

OSCAR: Well, first of all, we're going to TAGS. Mr Surridge needs me to help him work out how to tell the world about Luke's re-appearance. The optics need to be worked out very carefully.

BETH: But…what about lockdown?

OSCAR: We're going to break the rules.

BETH looks hesitant for a second, biting her lip. Then makes up her mind.

BETH: (*breathing deeply, calming herself*) Okay, yes. Rule-breaking. Yes, amazing! Bring it on!

OSCAR: (*approvingly*) What a profoundly diamond-cluster-deserving thing to say.

They exit together, holding hands.

SCENE 15

At the front of the stage are: NARRATOR, INSPECTOR COODE, SERGEANT WILDERSPIN, RICHARD MAGNUS, EVE SURRIDGE and GWEN LAPP, all with microphones in front of them, addressing a press conference. There's a large crowd of journalists, as well as camera crew, and spectators watching and listening.

NARR: September the 10th. Today, it has emerged that missing schoolboy Luke Surridge has been found alive and well. With the help of crime-solving fifteen-year-old Oscar Landrigan, Luke's father Derek Surridge found Luke six months ago…

Gasps of shock come from the crowd.

NARR: – that's right, six months ago. I'm afraid we have been unable to get an explanation from anyone involved about how precisely Luke came to be found, or where, or who had taken him in the first place, but we *can* confirm that Luke is safe and in good health. 'I've never felt better,' he told the family liaison officer who visited him as as soon as the authorities had been notified of his reappearance. Speaking for his client Derek Surridge, solicitor Richard Magnus said:

RICH M: On behalf of my client – the one who was so obviously innocent from the start – I would like to read the following statement. 'It's hard to summon the words to express how overjoyed I am that Luke has been found alive and well. I am immensely grateful to all the people who have stood by me: my brother and sister, Duncan and Diane, my solicitor Richard Magnus, my friend and colleague Oscar Landrigan, and all my other wrongly accused and loyal friends and colleagues at TAGS, who have been a tower of strength throughout this dark time.'

NARR: Inspector Oliver Coode of Cambridgeshire Police said…

INSP C: It saddens me greatly to hear that Derek Surridge has been flaunting his innocence privilege with no concern for the guilty community who, so often, are the ones who end up behind bars. For a non-criminal like Mr Surridge to use his considerable platform to boast of his innocence only demonstrates how far we still have to go if we wish to achieve equal outcomes for innocent and guilty alike.

NARR: Headteacher of Pffisham School, Gwen Lapp, said:

GWEN L: If Luke Surridge has been found safe and well, then there is no excuse for his not having been immediately returned to serve the rest of his sentence in Pffisham School's Detention Unit. I have lodged an official complaint, and will not let the matter rest until this injustice has been remedied.

NARR: Eve Surridge, Luke's mother and ex-wife of Derek Surridge, said:

EVE S: Everyone apart from me who ever believed my husband Derek was guilty ought to be ashamed of themselves. When I publicly disowned and slandered him, I didn't really mean it. Deep down, I knew he could never have harmed Luke. Now that our beloved son is back and TAGS is rumoured to be bringing in five million pounds a month, I believe Derek and I owe it to Luke to give our relationship and our family another chance.

Crowd boos her.

SCENE 16

TAGS offices. All TAGS STAFF are there, including the WRONGLY ACCUSED, DEREK SURRIDGE, DIANE SURRIDGE, DUNCAN SURRIDGE, OSCAR, ASBO, BETHANY and BARTIE VOSS and CLEMENCY and PETER LANDRIGAN. Also present is LUKE SURRIDGE. DEREK SURRIDGE stands with arm around his son, clearly overjoyed to be reunited with him.

CLEM: *(to PETER)* I can't believe it. Luke Surridge!

LUKE, hearing his name, waves at her. CLEM waves back.

CLEM: There he is, all in one piece and looking decidedly perky. Rather strange, given his years-long ordeal in captivity! Still, I suppose he was found six months ago, so he's had time to rehydrate. (*Peers more closely*) I wonder if he's had some cosmetic work done.

PETER: I smell a rat. I hope Oscar hasn't done anything dodgy.

CLEM: He hasn't, Peter. You've got to change the way you think about our son.

PETER: We'll see.

OSCAR: Ladies and gentleman, can I have your full attention, please? (*Clears his throat*) As we speak, a press conference is taking place at which the nation's media are being told that they will probably never find out who or what was behind Luke Surridge's strange disappearance all those years ago. Only a select few will ever know the truth – and that's you lot, so count yourselves lucky. You're about to get the full story.

CLEM: (*clutches PETER's arm*) Ooh, goody! The goss, at long last!

OSCAR: Now, I nearly invited someone else to this little gathering...Karen Beaton, host of the popular podcast 'Justice for Locked Room Luke'. In the end, I decided not to invite her.

DIANE: Quite right too! After the lies she told about Mr Surridge–

OSCAR: Ah, but they weren't lies. Karen Beaton told the truth *to the best of her recollection*. That's why her witness statement was so muddled, why she kept changing it. One minute it was both Mr Surridge and Luke in pyjamas, then she changed her story and suddenly it was only Luke in pyjamas. Human memory is an imperfect measure of anything. If she'd been lying, her account would have been more consistent. Less imaginative. I mean, she might have pretended to have seen Mr Surridge with Luke in his car, but would she really have invented pyjamas out of nowhere?

DIANE: But that's how I know she lied. Mr Surridge never used to wear pyjamas in the daytime before Luke went missing.

OSCAR: And Karen Beaton didn't see him wearing them the day Luke disappeared. She was quite right to change her statement - and yet, she did see what she thought she saw, in a way.

DUNCAN: Do you mean that Luke was wearing pyjamas?

LUKE S: But I wasn't!

OSCAR: No, you weren't. (*Walks slowly around the stage, enjoying the moment of almost-revelation*) In fact, nobody was wearing pyjamas. But you *were* in the car with your father that day, Luke. He didn't kidnap you – or murder you, obviously – but he did drive you away from school, after you *escaped* from the Detention Unit. I'm right, aren't I?

BARTIE: Escaped? You're saying Luke broke himself out of a locked room, with no help from anyone?

OSCAR: Oh, he had help. He couldn't have done it on his own – impossible. He had help from a certain…clay model of a French teacher. Monsieur LeClay – someone I'd never have thought of in connection with Luke's disappearance if it hadn't been for what Karen Beaton told us.

BETH: Oscar, you're not making sense.

LUKE S: (*impressed*) I've…honestly no idea how you worked that out, Oscar.

DUNCAN: You're…surely not confirming that he's correct, in front of…all these people?

LUKE S: Dunkle, the game's up. Evidently Oscar knows everything. We might as well come clean.

OSCAR: (*chuckles*) Dunkle! I like it. From Uncle Duncan, right?

LUKE S: (*to DUNCAN, astonished*) See? He literally knows everything.

OSCAR: Duncan, Diane…you've got nothing to worry about. No one here's going to say anything – to the police, to the papers. Relax. What's revealed at TAGS stays at TAGS.

(*Turns to his audience*) With the help of Monsieur LeClay, Luke managed to get out of the locked room he was in. He made a run for it, and as he did so, he must have seen his dad, Mr Surridge, getting into his car in the school car park after his meeting with the headmaster. (*Looks at LUKE for confirmation*)

LUKE nods.

OSCAR: Luke then did what teenagers all over the world do many times a day: he asked his dad for a lift.

LUKE S: And I told him that I was never, under any circumstances, going back to Pffisham, the Guantanamo Bay of Cambridge schools.

OSCAR: Exactly. *(To LUKE*) Good choice. (*To the assembled crowd*) This left Mr Surridge with a sizeable problem. He agreed with Luke, but neither of them was the boss in their house. Luke's mother was in charge of all decisions, major and minor: Eve Surridge. And she either believed, or insisted on pretending, that Pffisham was a brilliant school. Mr Surridge knew she'd force Luke back there, only to be locked up again, and he didn't have the nerve to defy her, so, in desperation…(*Turns to MR SURRIDGE*) I'm guessing you went to Diane and Duncan for help?

MR S: (*proud, impressed*) You guess correctly, young Oscar.

OSCAR: You knew you couldn't hide Luke yourself, or know where he was, or see him. You couldn't have any contact with him at all – you'd have felt too guilty, knowing your wife had lost her child. You felt duty-bound to share that loss, since you'd created it. Also, you couldn't trust yourself with the knowledge of where Luke could be found - you suspected you'd blurt it out to your wife one day, when her unhappiness, and yours, became too much to bear. The only way Luke could be kept safely away from Pffisham, you decided, was if Diane and Duncan handled it all and kept you in the dark. Which they agreed to do. Luke has probably been staying at one of their houses all this time. (*To his audience*) Selflessly, Mr Surridge put himself through the agony of having no contact with Luke for years in order to rescue him from the terrible fate of remaining a Pffishamian. Oh – (*for those who don't know*) that's what Pffisham School calls its pupils.

MR S: And I knew I couldn't endure it for much longer, Oscar. That's why I asked for your help in…well, in finding Luke and ending my long and horrible ordeal. I thought there could be no way out for me, Diane or Duncan that wouldn't involve public shaming and horrible punishments, but you've ingeniously created a way out: all of us in this room now simply agree never to tell anyone the truth. Genius! (*He frowns suddenly*) Though it's a shame Karen Beaton can't be included in our little gang. I must admit, I have a soft spot for Karen. If it weren't for her, the idea of wearing pyjamas in the daytime would never have occurred to me, and it's so much more comfortable than wearing actual clothes.

BARTIE: Speaking of ways out, and pyjamas… If we can return to the matter of Monsieur LeClay…

CLEM: Oh, yes, do let's! I'm dying to hear how an inanimate clay teacher helped Luke escape from captivity.

OSCAR: Luke, do you want to take it from here?

LUKE S: I'd rather hear it from you, Oscar. I still can't believe you worked it out.

OSCAR: Fine. Okay, so, picture the scene: there was Luke, newly locked up in the Detention Unit by sadist Gwen Lapp. Now, in those days – until the school threw him away, after the newspapers exposed the scandal – Monsieur LeClay used to hang out in the Detention Unit at least two days a week. Gwen Lapp and other teachers would use him to gaslight incarcerated children. 'Look, you're not on your own,' they'd say. 'You've got Monsieur LeClay here to keep you company.'

Shocked gasps break out all over.

OSCAR: Yeah, I know. Pure evil. But it's true. I was often locked away with LeClay. Luke would have been too. I only realised when I was told that ASBO had been *completely alone* in that room apart from a green chicken on a tray–

ASBO: (*smiling, as if at a fond memory*) That chicken was a bro. I still feel bad for leaving him behind.

OSCAR: I realised: of course, no more Monsieur LeClay, because the school felt pressured to get rid of him – but that happened long after Luke disappeared. So, I thought, it stands to reason that LeClay could well have been locked in that room with Luke, at least some of the time. As a so-called companion.

LUKE: He was.

OSCAR: Right. So *then* I put that together with Karen Beaton's story about the pyjamas... And now, ladies and gentlemen, you can all join in this next part. Who's got their phone with them? Everyone, yeah? Good. Get them out.

CLEM: What's the WiFi password for TAGS, Oscar?

OSCAR: There's no time for that, Mum. Use 5G.

(*CATHY and JEN exchange shocked gasps at this suggestion*)

ASBO: (*pulling out his new iPhone, holding it up in the air proudly. Sings under his breath to tune of 'Windows All Locked Firmly'…*) For I have been promised a brand new iPhone!

OSCAR: I'd like you all to put into the search box 'Blue and white striped pyjamas'. That's what Karen Beaton said she saw, on either Derek Surridge or Luke Surridge or both. Now, click on 'Images' and you'll notice that in almost all of the pictures, the blue of the pyjamas is sky blue - pale blue. Agreed?

Everyone murmurs their strong agreement.

OSCAR: Right. But that's not what Karen Beaton saw. She described thick navy stripes on a white background – the very thing someone might choose to put on a clay model that they wanted to pass off as a Frenchman. Put 'typical Frenchman attire' into your search boxes and see what comes up.

Everyone obeys this instruction and then gasps in recognition.

CLEM: Oh, my goodness, Peter, he's right! White tunic with thick navy horizontal stripes – that's everyone's idea of the classic French top, isn't it?

BETH: (*to OSCAR*) You're…you're saying that Luke dressed as Monsieur LeClay before escaping from the locked room?

OSCAR: Precisely. (*Proudly*) That's my brilliant fiancée Beth who just worked that out, everyone. I think this is what must have happened: Luke was sitting there, feeling quite desperate and wondering how to escape, when he heard some teachers coming up the stairs. Perhaps from their conversation as they approached the locked door, he worked out that they were coming for LeClay – maybe he was due to fake-teach a French class. Thinking quickly, Luke dressed LeClay in his own school uniform and dressed himself in LeClay's clothes, including that typical French dude top. He then let himself be carried to a classroom and left there, and as soon as the teachers had gone, but before any pupils had arrived, he scarpered.

LUKE: Correct.

OSCAR: Now, of course, Evil Gwen Lapp was the one who claimed to have found the locked room *empty* when she went to check on Luke shortly after imprisoning him – but we know she's a liar. That's a proven fact.

ASBO: She lied about me throwing my pencil case at her face.

OSCAR: And she lied by omission when she failed to tell the police that she'd found LeClay in the Detention Unit, dressed in Luke's school uniform. She knew it would make the school look terrible if she admitted that a member of the notorious Reprobate gang had been allowed to undress a French teacher – even a pretend one.

(*There's a loud knock at the door*)

OSCAR: Er…come in?

Enter LYNDA TERRY from the county council, wearing a mask.

LYNDA: (*removing her mask*) I knew it! Oscar Landrigan! You have no right to be here.

MR S: Yes, he does. He works here. Officially, now.

LYNDA: He is urgently needed by the 'Yuck! Boys!' programme. We still don't have anyone else with a famous murdered romantic novelist grandmother. (*In desperation*) Look, I've been told that if I fail to enlist him, I'll be fired.

OSCAR: I'm going nowhere, Mrs Terry. And…I mean, do you really care if you lose your job? Jobs aren't much fun – except here at TAGS. Being employed here is *amazing*.

WENDY: Thanks to *you*, Oscar!

BETH: TAGS is where everyone wants to work these days, even me and Bartie. It's so dynamic and imaginative!

JEN: It's true! We so look forward to each new day here at TAGS, knowing Oscar is leading us to ever-greater achievement and success!

CLEM: (*digs PETER in the ribs*) You see, Peter?

PETER: How extraordinary!

SONG NO. 20: THE DAY OF THE WONDERFUL BOY

All TAGS STAFF sing:

One More Day
(As they say),
One more day for us all to enjoy!
Hip hooray!
Every day
Is the day of the wonderful boy!

Oscar's turned us around.
Thanks to him, we have found
Our true calling in life, and the day never drags.
Brand new start, brand new dawn,
And no more need to warn
Anyone they'd be crazy to work here at TAGS,

Where no pain
Can remain
Where there's pure satisfaction and joy!
So we say
Hip hooray!
It's the day of the wonderful boy!

WENDY sings:

We were wrongly accused
By the deeply confused,
The deluded and dim, the corrupt and unfair.
Do we mind? Not a bit!
We're obliged to admit
That we wouldn't have…

PAUL: *(spoken)…otherwise….*

WENDY: *....ended up here.*

ALL sing:

What's a frown?
Not a noun
For a person in TAGS's employ.
Here we say
Every day
Is the day of the wonderful boy.
Hip hooray,
It's the day,
It's the day of the wonderful boy!

OSCAR: Maybe you'd like to work here too, Mrs T? We can afford to pay you way more than the council does.

LYNDA: Well...it sounds lovely, but...I'm afraid I don't entirely understand the nature of the work.

CLEM: (*to PETER*) Neither do I, Peter – but I'm going to work for TAGS anyway. It sounds heavenly. And I'm sick to the back teeth of beastly perfumes.

CATHY: Oh, our company's mission isn't hard get to grips with once you've read Oscar's brilliant business plan. He's written it all out very clearly: the firm's whole ethos. Look... (*She produces a piece of paper, hands it to LYNDA*).

LYNDA: This is...very different from anything I've ever seen at a County Council meeting.

JEN: That's because Oscar's a true original. We've all learned the TAGS mission statement by heart. Listen – soon you'll have it by heart too...

SONG NO. 21: LET'S PRETEND TO BE HEROES

JEN sings:

What if we say that we're heroes
Even if no one agrees?
Ignore the concerned dear-oh-dear-ohs.
If the business is down on its knees,
Let's picture at least seven zeros
On a cheque that we'll soon be receiving.
Let's all pretend to be heroes
And let's get the whole world believing.

TAGS STAFF sing:

What if we say that we're heroes?
Even if deep down, we doubt it.
Our huge profit margin this year shows
That there's something quite brilliant about it.
Can you picture a cool seven zeros
On a cheque that you'll soon be receiving?
Let's all pretend to be heroes
And let's get the whole world believing.

OSCAR, CLEM, PETER, ASBO, BARTIE, BETH AND LYNDA sing:

Let's all pretend that we're heroes.
Perhaps we can make it come true.
Gavin Williamsons, Robert De Niros
Might have once been like me and like you.
Let's all put on hero disguises
And wear them as long as we can.
Let's accept all the tributes and prizes.
Maybe that's how all heroes began.

ALL sing:

Let's act like we're heroes and winners
And if we find that we've lost our way
Like a bunch of imposter-beginners,
Let's practise what we'll need to say:
That we can still be heroes,
We'll pretend to be heroes,
We're bound to be heroes someday.
So believe in your heroes! Stay true to your heroes!
Add you *to your heroes toda-a-ay!*
We'll make brand new heroes. We all can be heroes.
We're bound to be heroes someda-a-ay!

THE END